ELSEVIER ARCHITECTURAL SCIENCE SERIES

Editor

HENRY J. COWAN

Professor of Architectural Science
University of Sydney

Previously published

An Historical Outline of Architectural Science
by H. J. COWAN

Thermal Performance of Buildings
by J. F. VAN STRAATEN

Fundamental Foundations
by W. FISHER CASSIE

Computers in Architectural Design
by D. CAMPION

In press

Principles of Natural Lighting
by J. A. LYNES

Electrical Services in Buildings
by P. JAY AND J. HEMSLEY

Models in Architecture

by

H. J. COWAN, J. S. GERO, G. D. DING

Department of Architectural Science, University of Sydney

and

R. W. MUNCEY

Commonwealth Scientific and Industrial Research Organization
Melbourne

ELSEVIER PUBLISHING COMPANY

AMSTERDAM — LONDON — NEW YORK

1968

ELSEVIER PUBLISHING COMPANY LIMITED
BARKING, ESSEX, ENGLAND

ELSEVIER PUBLISHING COMPANY
335 JAN VAN GALENSTRAAT, P.O. BOX 211, AMSTERDAM
THE NETHERLANDS

AMERICAN ELSEVIER PUBLISHING COMPANY INC.
52 VANDERBILT AVENUE, NEW YORK, N.Y 10017

LIBRARY OF CONGRESS CATALOG CARD NUMBER 68-17576

WITH 98 ILLUSTRATIONS AND 6 TABLES

© 1968 ELSEVIER PUBLISHING COMPANY LIMITED

Printed in Great Britain by Galliard Limited, Great Yarmouth, England

Preface

Models have been used in architectural design for as long as buildings have been planned systematically. Visual demonstration of form has been their main function; but recently greater emphasis has been given to problems of planning, structural behaviour, lighting, ventilation and acoustics. Quantitative assessment is used to an increasing extent due to the improvement of instruments after the Second World War.

The authors have endeavoured to describe both the quantitative and the qualitative use of models in architectural design. Some techniques of experimental stress analysis are mentioned only briefly because their successful application has been in the design of dams, aeroplanes or machines, rather than buildings. This book thus excludes some material normally covered in texts on structural model analysis, but includes visual and environmental models.

Most of the examples are drawn from Australia, partly because details were readily available, and partly because this may help to correct an imbalance in the existing literature, which is mainly confined to buildings in Europe or America. The authors are indebted to Mr. P. Balint, Dr. L. K. Stevens, and Mr. P. R. Tregenza for particulars of models tested by them. They would like to express their appreciation to Mr. John Dixon and the Department of Illustration, Sydney University, for taking the photographs, to Mr. Hans Milton, B.Arch., M.Bdg.Sc., and Mr. P. L. Andrews, B.Arch., for preparing the drawings, and to Mrs. Rita Arthurson, Miss Edwina Dight and Mrs. Ann Moravec for typing the manuscript. Finally, they would like to thank Mr. John Dixon, Chief Laboratory Technician, and the technical staff of the Department of Architectural Science for help with the models made and tested at the University of Sydney.

Sydney, June 1968   H.J.C.
                                                          J.S.G.

Dedicated to the laboratory technicians without whose aid no model analysis would be possible

Contents

Chapter 1

The Significance of Model Analysis for the Design of Buildings

1.1. The Special Problems of the Building Industry

Building differs from most other manufacturing industries. Its products are quite expensive, but generally only one article is made to each design. Disastrous failures are not likely, and design is therefore comparatively superficial. The cost of designing a building is between 5 to 10 per cent of the total; and the cost of designing the structure, which is most amenable to model analysis, is of the order of 1 per cent of the total cost of the building. It is often preferable to use an approximate calculation than to employ a precise analysis.

This is not true in the design of most other commodities. The cost of designing a plastic case for a radio receiver is many times the cost of a single receiver. This is not important because a great many receivers are made to a single design.

By comparison, the number of aeroplanes produced to a single design is small. Aeroplanes must be very light. To achieve this, they are designed with a low factor of structural safety, and the cost of design may eventually be a large part of the cost of the aeroplane; however, this is unavoidable if the plane is to operate economically.

A dam retaining the water in a reservoir is a compact form of structure, and an expensive one. Its shape is largely determined by the shape of the surrounding rock. Although it is a one-off structure, model analysis is extensively employed because it is a small item in the cost, because failure would be disastrous, and because the shape is so irregular that theoretical solutions are complex.

None of these arguments apply to the design of buildings. We cannot afford to break a complete full-size architectural structure as we can break a prototype plastic radio casing. We need not design it with as low a factor of safety as in aircraft design; although weight costs money, a concrete floor with excessive structural depth may help with sound insulation and fire protection, and ultimately prove

1

economical. If the structure is misdesigned, it will usually show signs of distress in good time, while the aeroplane may disintegrate in mid-air. If the shape proves mathematically too complex, we can change it, whereas we cannot change the boundaries of a dam. The simplified geometry of the building may look a little different from the original concept, but a good deal of latitude is possible within the framework of modern mathematical techniques.

Many of the techniques used in the model analysis of architectural structures are derived from the general manufacturing industry, the aircraft industry, and from the design of dams (*see* Section 2.11); not all are economical when applied to buildings.

The problems are much the same in other aspects of building design. We can use models for the design of the acoustic, lighting and thermal environment, but these have remained research, rather than design tools, partly because most of the problems are amenable to calculation, even if approximate, and partly because there is a substantial tolerance of error. If a concert-hall falls down, something has to be done about it; if its acoustics are poor, we may put up with them for a century.

It is perhaps in its least scientific aspects that the architectural model has so far been most successful. Most architects use a model to show the appearance of the building. These models are generally viewed from above, *i.e.* the point of view of an observer in an aeroplane, and consequently do not convey a correct impression. This defect could be readily corrected with a small periscope; but few people use one. The model is a means of explaining the architectural concept to the layman; it helps the architect to visualize the entire scheme; it is rarely used for detailed architectural design, which is done on paper.

This aspect of model design has not been considered sufficiently in architectural science. Even where a structural model may not be the best means of obtaining the detailed dimensions of a structure, it can often help the architect and his client, and often also the structural consultant, to obtain a better appreciation of the problem. Much the same applies to models of lighting and ventilation.

The inter-relation of the various forms of model analysis also has not received sufficient attention. Thus a complex roof-shape needs to be tested in a wind-tunnel to obtain the distribution of wind-pressure and suction, since there is virtually no theoretical solution to this problem if the shape departs much from simple geometry. A model of the roof shape, with holes for measuring wind-pressure, forms an excellent mould to make a plastic model for structural analysis, and the cost of the latter is reduced accordingly. It is often possible to use architectural or structural models for a lighting analysis, if this point is considered initially, and so on. Model analysis could therefore be more economical if the various aspects were considered together initially, with due allowance for the scale factors appropriate to various forms of analysis.

The main obstacle to the wider use of models in architectural science, however, is the rapid advance of theory.

1.2. Experiment versus Theory

Theoretical and experimental analysis are essentially complementary forms of structural design. Advances in theory tend to reduce reliance on experimental solutions, and *vice versa*.

Models were occasionally used in the Middle Ages and the Renaissance. Domenico Fontana describes in his published account of the erection of the obelisk outside St. Peter's in Rome, how he designed the layout of the hoisting ropes with a model lead obelisk; but there are no fully authenticated examples of model analysis for the structural design of buildings from that period.

In the late 18th century the elastic theory made rapid progress, and iron was used more and more for structural design in the next few decades. Empirical rules gave way to theoretical calculations, and structural systems were adapted to the existing simple theory. Before the 20th century the theory of structures was never used successfully for the design of complex masonry vaults and domes, which continued to be designed by empirical rules.

The growing sophistication of structural theory was largely responsible for the increasing complexity of engineered structures in the 20th century. This encouraged the search for a mechanized form of structural design as calculations became more laborious.

The apparatus devised by Beggs at Princeton University in 1922, the first successful method of model analysis, and other early examples may be regarded as mechanical analogues of the elastic theory, rather than scale models of a part of the building. Their significance lay in the fact that they gave the same answer as the mathematical solution; it was incidental that the model dimensions were proportional to those of the structure.

In other fields of engineering the theory of dimensional analysis was well established in the early 20th century. Scale models were regularly used for hydraulic works, and in the 1920's wind-tunnels were commonly employed to test scale models of aeroplanes and aeroplane parts.

The techniques of structural model analysis were greatly improved during the same period; but the significant development of the early 1930's was the invention of the *Moment-Distribution Method* by Cross, which made the design of linear rigid frames much simpler by calculation.

At the same time imaginative reinforced concrete structures of complex shape began to make their appearance in Southern Europe. Both Nervi and Torroja used small scale models in their designs. During the Second World War aircraft design made great progress, and structural design of aeroplanes with the aid of scale models instrumented with the new miniature electric resistance strain gauges was carried to a high degree of perfection. In the late 1940's the method was applied to architectural structures, and rapid design solutions were obtained for problems hitherto soluble only by exceedingly lengthy calculations.

The Second World War had produced another powerful design tool which took a little longer to be adapted to structural design. In the 1950's digital computer solutions for structural problems became available, and the scope of computer-based design is steadily increasing. If the picture had altered rapidly in favour of model design, it now shifted again the other way.

The rapid change has been caused by remarkable progress in structural analysis. Opinions may differ on the aesthetic merits of the "Architecture of Structural Excitement"; but there is little doubt about the technical advances. The patterns of Beggs' Apparatus available in 1965 are superior to the original 1922 version; but we have better techniques of design, and this form of model analysis is now obsolete.

Is structural model analysis then merely an historical interlude? Clearly the authors would not have taken the trouble to write a book on models, unless they considered that they had a definite place in architectural design. For a proper assessment we must take account of two other aspects. One is the realism of model design. The true scale model, unlike the digital computer, is more than a structural analogue. It can copy the exact degree of rigidity, the continuity of adjacent structural members, and the irregular openings which architectural planning may demand. These can be incorporated only with difficulty in a mathematical solution.

The second factor is the new importance of the non-specialist, and the growing use of model techniques for other aspects of architectural design (visual models, environmental models, etc.). The client's point of view is not merely important because he pays the bill. He often has an unrivalled knowledge of the requirements of the building, and he can thus help the architect and the specialist consultants, if he understands their problems. The architect, in turn, cannot be expected to know the details of structural theory, and the various consultants may be equally unfamiliar with one another's specialities. At the present time, computer programs are no help to understanding the problems of other experts. Models, however, are frequently simple enough to be readily intelligible. If the concept of the integrated design of the building is to become accepted, communication of ideas will need to be greatly improved. The value of model analysis cannot be measured merely by comparing the cost of a theoretical solution for a given set of boundary conditions with that of a model solution for the same boundary conditions. We must also enquire whether we can express the boundary conditions in mathematical terms, and whether we can explain the result to all members of the design team who should understand the implications.

The next Chapter gives an historical survey of the principal model and analogue techniques, and assumes familiarity with structural theory. Readers who are interested mainly in immediately useful methods are recommended to turn to Chapter 4.

Chapter 2

A Survey of the Development of Modern Methods of Structural Model Analysis

2.1. Structural Design before the 20th Century

The first accurate data on the strength of structures were obtained by full-scale experimentation before there was a useful theory. Galileo in *Two New Sciences* [2.1] was able to give an experimental result for the strength of a cantilever, but not a correct theoretical answer; it took another century and a half to obtain a correct theoretical solution [2.2].

During the 18th century experimental data on ultimate strength were accumulated, frequently by the simple, if laborious method of hanging heavy weights from full-size structural members (Fig. 2.1). Experimental elasticity could not develop until the necessary strain

Fig. 2.1. Bending test by direct loading. (From *An Essay on the Strength and Stress of Timber*, by Peter Barlow. Printed for A. J. Taylor at the Architectural Library, London 1817. Plate V.)

measuring devices became available in the late 19th century, and only failure could be determined accurately [2.4]. The experimental results consequently did not agree with the existing theory, which was based on elasticity. The discrepancy was most serious with timber and wrought iron which are subject to appreciable stress redistribution before failure; but even brittle materials, like natural stone and cast iron, show inelastic deformation.

By the early 19th century theoretical knowledge was well ahead of experiment. When Navier published *Résumé des Leçons* in 1826, engineers received for the first time a systematic presentation of an elastic theory of structural design.

Progress in model analysis was much slower, because few instruments existed before 1870 for measuring strains. While numerous precision instruments were developed in the following two decades, capable of measuring strains of about 10^{-5}, and some of these are still in use today, most of the early instruments were too delicate for use on actual structures; the Howard gauge (Fig. 2.2) was a pioneer in the field.

Fig. 2.2. The Howard strain gauge, 1888. The relative movement of the two gauge points was measured through coaxial tubes with a screw micrometer to an accuracy of 0·0001 inches. Two men were required for satisfactory operation.

Tests on full-scale structures have always been difficult and expensive. Experiments with small-scale models were impossible before the development of light-weight extensometers with small gauge lengths; the first was the *miniature compound-lever tensometer* developed by Huggenberger in the 1920's. Three-dimensional model analysis made real progress only after the invention of bonded, electric-resistance strain-gauges in the late 1930's.

Experimental techniques were most successful in the 19th century for the solution of buckling problems. The emphasis in France at the time was on theory, while the English approach during the same period was more empirical. The solutions were often less elegant, but some important results not predicted by the existing theory were obtained by systematic observation. Easton Hodgkinson's experiments on columns in 1840 formed the basis of Gordon's and Rankine's empirical column formulae, superseded by theoretical solutions only at the turn of the century. In 1848 Hodgkinson tested 1/7 scale models of the tubular girders for the Conway Railway Bridge [2.3], and discovered the buckling of compression flanges.

During the entire 19th century, however, the emphasis remained on theory.

2.2. Structures Become Statically Indeterminate

In 1870 Castigliano gave the first general solution for the design of statically indeterminate structures [2.5], which is still considered an admirable method for the solution of rigid arches. The invention of the structural steel skeleton in Chicago in the 1880's [2.6] focussed attention on the design of multi-storey rigid frames, and Castigliano's strain energy method is too laborious for their design. Following the adoption of reinforced concrete for multi-storey buildings, the problem of rigid frame design became acute because of the greater rigidity of concrete joints. The development of *slope deflection methods* by Bendixen and Maney in 1914 provided a more convenient tool. They also emphasised the significance of the deformation of the structure in the evaluation of the statically indeterminate forces, and the first successful methods of model analysis were all based on elastic deformations.

2.3. Indirect Model Analysis by Müller–Breslau's Principle

Beggs devised his *deformeter* at Princeton University in 1922 [2.7]. It is the first of a number of methods based on a theorem which relates the deformations caused at a support and at some point along the structure to the magnitude of the respective forces. Thus if we consider the beam in Fig. 2.3, and give it a displacement δ_A at A, thus producing a displacement δ_B at B, then it can be shown by

Müller–Breslau's theorem [2.9] that the reaction R_A produced at A by a force W_B at B is given by

$$R_A . \delta_A = W_B . \delta_B.$$

If we apply a unit deformation at A and measure the resulting deformation at some point along the beam, B, this is numerically equal to the statically indeterminate reaction at A caused by a unit load at B. This means that the shape of the deflected member is the influence line* for the reaction.

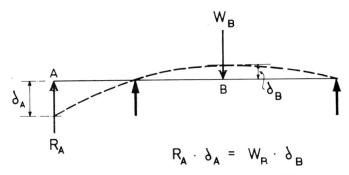

Fig. 2.3. Muller–Breslau's theorem. It can be shown [2.9] that:
$$R_A . \delta_A = W_B . \delta_B.$$

Beggs devised equipment for producing accurately very small unit displacements (Fig. 2.4). He used a micrometer microscope to measure the resulting deformations along the members of the structure. The use of the microscope produced a good deal of eyestrain, and the accuracy of the cardboard models employed by Beggs in his first experiments left much to be desired. (Celluloid was later used with better results.)

It has since been shown that the small displacements are not normally necessary [2.8]. The first of the large-displacement methods is the *Continostat* of Otto Gottschalk [2.10]. Displacements could be

---

* The influence line is the curve showing the variation of some quantity (say an unknown reaction) due to a unit load travelling along the beam. In this case the influence line at some point B shows the magnitude of the reaction R_A due to a unit load W_B acting on the beam at B.

measured with an ordinary scale, and steel was used for the models, which avoided the error caused by the non-uniformity of cardboard or by the creep of celluloid. Like Begg's apparatus, it was produced commercially; but neither became important as a design tool.

The main defect of the Continostat was the restriction which the number of fabricated sections, with a limited range of sectional properties, imposed on design. This was also a limitation of the apparatus, called the *Nupabest*, described by Rieckhoff in *Experimentelle Statik* (Darmstadt, 1927).

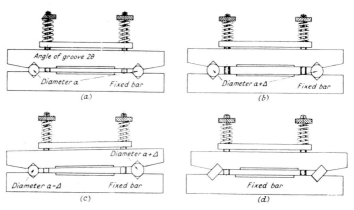

Fig. 2.4. Begg's apparatus for producing unit displacements (after Pippard). (a) No displacement, (b) unit vertical displacement for thrust influence line, (c) unit angular displacement for bending moment influence line, (d) unit horizontal displacement for shear influence line.

Eney's *Deformeter* [2.11] combines the easy machinability of celluloid (or some other plastic) with the use of large deformations, and it is the best of the designs mentioned so far. There are several other methods, improving on the original ideas, of more recent date (B 1, 3, and 4). In the meantime, however, Cross had developed the *Moment Distribution Method* for calculating rigid frames, and indirect model analysis was thus outmoded before it had been fully perfected.

Cross' theoretical method is not suitable for the design of arches and other curved structures. While the indirect method of model analysis can be used, it is liable to serious errors. The model gives the moment due to the statically indeterminate reactions, M_r. The net bending moment is

$$M = M_w - M_r$$

where M_w is the statically determinate bending moment due to the loads. In arches, both M_w and M_r may be very much larger than M (Fig. 2.5). This is, of course, the reason for the efficiency of arches in bridging large spans, since the arch effect (M_r) reduces the moment corresponding to a simply supported beam (M_w). However, in the design of the arch, we face the difficulty that the unavoidable small error of the model analysis in determining M_r may be multiplied many times in the subtraction.

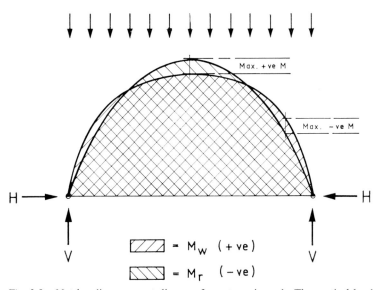

Fig. 2.5. Net bending moment diagram for a two-pin arch. The vertical load acting on the arch and the vertical reactions at the support produce a statically determinate positive bending moment M_w. The moment due to the horizontal reaction ($= H \times$ rise of arch) is negative and statically indeterminate; it may be obtained by model analysis. The net bending moment is the difference between the two

$$M = M_w - M_r$$

it can be either positive or negative. Great precision may be needed in the determination of M_r if the maximum net bending moments are not to be seriously in error.

The errors resulting from the creep of plastic models while the measurements are taken, and the labour of individual measurements with a scale model, can be reduced by making two exposures on the same photograph, one before displacement and one afterwards [2.12]. For uniformly distributed loads, the reactions may be obtained by measuring the displaced area with a planimeter.

Indirect model analysis can be used, in principle, for three-dimensional structures. This has been done at least three times. A beamless staircase was analyzed by applying displacements in three dimensions to the supports [2.13], and this proved a very expensive method. An indirect model analysis of a braced dome [2.14] by altering the length of individual members by a known amount has been more economical. Pippard analysed the bow-girder ramp of the Penguin Pool at the London Zoo, an unusual but very small structure, with an indirect model (B 3) without the use of fully three-dimensional displacements.

The increasing range of computer programs makes it unlikely that indirect model analysis will prove a useful design tool in the foreseeable future. As a teaching aid, however, it retains an important place. It illustrates an important structural principle, and in the

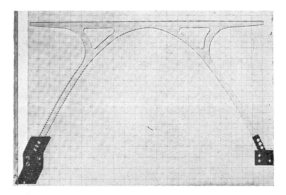

Fig. 2.6. Apparatus for indirect model analysis for large displacements. The fixing device at the end of the arch is capable of a horizontal or vertical displacement of $\pm \frac{1}{2}$ inch for determining the horizontal and vertical reactions, and a rotation of $\pm \frac{1}{4}$ radian (14° 18′) for determining fixing moments. The displacement along the arch is measured by drawing its outline on squared paper before and after moving the fixing device. (*Architectural Science Laboratory, University of Sydney.*)

light of the knowledge gained we can now obtain results satisfactory for instruction with very simple tools (Fig. 2.6).

2.4. Model Analysis by Direct Loading and Indirect Strain Measurement

In the indirect method, described in Section 2.3, the model is given a unit deformation at a selected point, and the deformations elsewhere are measured to deduce the forces acting on the structure; these are then used to determine stresses. In the direct method, described in Sections 2.9 to 2.11, the model is given a load according to its scale factors, and the strains are measured directly; the stresses are deduced from the strains. Section 2.4 deals with models which are loaded, rather than deformed; but the strains are deduced indirectly from slopes and/or deflections; the method has been described as direct in papers primarily concerned with indirect model analysis, and as indirect in papers primarily concerned with direct model analysis.

The earliest suggestion for this approach appears to have been made by Coker [2.15]; the best-known instrument is the *Moment Indicator* developed at M.I.T. by Ruge [2.16].

When using models made of plastics, the problem of creep* during the progress of the test must be considered. With direct loading and indirect strain measurement, the change in the shape

---

* Metals stressed well below the yield or proof stress exhibit only elastic deformation. When the material is loaded, it deforms instantly, and the whole elastic deformation is recovered instantly on unloading.

Concrete, timber and plastics all exhibit creep to a larger or smaller extent, even at quite small stresses. When the material is loaded, the elastic deformation occurs immediately. The creep appears gradually; it may continue at a noticeable rate after several hours, or even days. The total deformation due to creep is usually more than the elastic deformation. When the material is unloaded, only the elastic deformation is recovered instantly.

When a model is given a fixed deformation, its shape does not change due to creep. Consequently, creep compensation is not essential in indirect model analysis, since measurements of the deformed shape can be made without difficulty. Owing to creep, however, the effective modulus of the plastic changes during the experiment, and consequently the external and internal forces change likewise with time. This complicates the interpretation of the results, and the more refined indirect models have included a compensating spring balance made from the same material as the model.

When a model is given a fixed load, its shape changes due to creep, because the model continues to deform as creep develops. Since creep is roughly proportional to stress, which varies in different parts of the model, the model continues to change its shape so long as creep continues.

of the model due to creep during the progress of the test becomes a
serious source of error, and a compensating spring balance made from
the same material as the model should be used (B 4).

The pointers attached to the Moment Indicator measure the
slopes (Fig. 2.7), and from them the bending moments are derived
by the Winkler equations also used in the *slope-deflection* and
moment-distribution theory:

$$M_{AB} = (2\theta_A + \theta_B).2EI/l$$

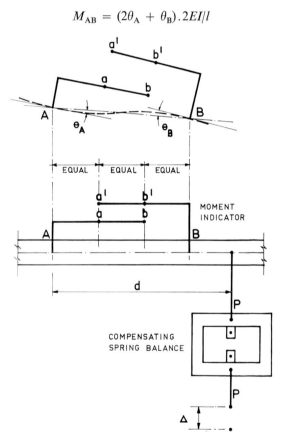

Fig. 2.7. Ruge's moment indicator. Two arms are attached to the member AB
of the structural model. As the model is loaded, the pointers rotate through the
same angles as the tangents of the member at the points A and B. The slopes θ_A
and θ_B can therefore be deduced from the movement of the pointers.

where M_{AB} is the bending moment in AB at A, θ is the slope, E is the modulus of elasticity, I the second moment of area, and l the span.

There are several other mechanical devices based on the same principle (B 4), and like the moment indicator they have no significant advantage over the indirect method. There are, however, a number of interesting variations. In a civil engineering laboratory with equipment for photogrammetric surveying, the deformations over a large surface can be obtained quickly with the camera [2.17]. The method has not been used sufficiently to assess its economic potential.

The Presan Corporation in California developed a method of *photo-reflective stress analysis* [2.18] specifically for the design of reinforced concrete flat-plate structures. A scale model is made from lucite (perspex) and its surface is silver-coated. A grid of parallel lines is then reflected in the model's mirror surface, distorted by the scaled load applied to it by an air bag. The distortions are measured by photographing the reflection of the grids, and these yield the strains on the mirrored surface. From them the radii of curvature, and hence the bending moments, are computed. The method became obsolete with the development of better theoretical methods of flat-plate design.

2.5. The Moiré Method

The *Moiré* method is basically another variation of model analysis by direct loading and indirect strain measurement. It has, however, a number of significant advantages over the older mechanical methods, and it gives a visual image of stress distribution which can greatly help the designer in the initial stages. The Moiré patterns are produced by interference between two series of lines, an undistorted parallel grid, and a similar grid distorted by the loaded model. This can be achieved either by reflection from the surface of the model, in a manner similar to the photo-reflective analysis (*see* Section 2.4), or by refraction, *i.e.* the light passing through the model. The reflective Moiré method, invented by Ligtenberg [2.19]

16   MODELS IN ARCHITECTURE

is the older, but the refractive variation, developed by Durelli [2.20], is the simpler of the two (Fig. 2.8). In Ligtenberg's technique two photographs for two distinct loading conditions (one usually zero loading) are superimposed on the same film by an intentional double exposure (the surface of the model is mirrored and the reflections of the ruled grid are reflected into the camera). de Jong, of the Delft Technological University, has compared the two methods [2.21].

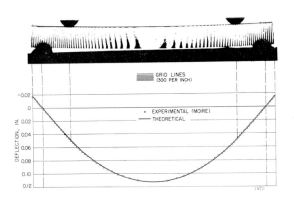

DEFLECTION LINE OF SIMPLY SUPPORTED BEAM UNDER PURE BENDING
OBTAINED BY MEANS OF MOIRE FRINGES AND THEORY (A. J. DURELLI)

Fig. 2.8.   Moiré fringes in a simply supported beam [2.20]. The beam, 1 inch deep and 12 inches long, is machined from Plexiglas, and has a grid of 300 lines per inch printed on it. The grid lines are parallel to the axis of the beam. A similarly printed plate is held in contact with the beam such that no fringes appear at zero load. When the load is applied, the model grid moves with respect to the fixed-in-space master grid, and the above fringe pattern appears. The fringe orders start from zero at the supports and increase towards the centre. One fringe order corresponds to 1/300 inch of displacement. The deflection curve of the beam can thus be plotted. (*By courtesy of Professor A. J. Durelli.*)

Both techniques can be used to measure slopes, and consequently curvature. In analysing a plate (for which the Moiré method is best suited), the fringe patterns for the two axes at right angles are found, and the bending moments are then obtained by graphical differentiation. The process is therefore far from direct; but in contrast to some of the other techniques, the spacing of the fringes gives an immediate visual impression.

The method has been used for shells of single curvature, but the membrane stresses affect the fringe patterns only if they cause a change in curvature. To obtain a complete picture, local strain gauges, photo-elasticity or micro-grids are needed in addition.

2.6. Micro-grids

A rectangular grid, say of fine rubber thread, cast into a transparent model shows up the elastic distortion due to membrane stresses [2.22]. The method is generally not sensitive without excessive distortion, but it can be a useful supplement to Moiré or photo-elastic patterns in structures subject to both membrane and bending stresses.

2.7. Photoelasticity

While there is a superficial similarity between photo-elasticity and Moiré patterns, the two methods are basically different. One yields slopes, the other differences between principal stresses.* Photoelastic fringes have for some time fascinated architects, because of their interesting patterns and brilliant colour, and many have seen a significance in them for the creation of new forms of architectural structures which they do not possess. Moiré patterns have not received the same attention, perhaps largely because they are still relatively unknown outside a small professional circle.

In 1816 Sir David Brewster published an observation that clear, strained glass exhibited coloured patterns when examined in polarized light. In 1850 Clerk Maxwell, in a paper *On the equilibrium of elastic solids*, read to the Royal Society of Edinburgh, explained the phenomenon and compared it with theoretical isochromatics. He also observed the dark bands produced by the isoclinics. Mesnager used photoelasticity for checking stress distribution around a load concentration. The real initiative came from Coker, whose book is still considered a standard work (B 6).

---

* Reference may be made to a text-book on the *Theory of Structures* or the *Strength of Materials* for the interpretation [*e.g.* 2.25]. The slope is proportional to the integral of the bending moment. The difference between the principal stresses is proportional to the maximum shear stress.

Photoelasticity is based on the property of certain transparent materials to break up the incident light into two components polarized in the directions of the principal stresses. Light waves are ordinarily oriented at random. By inserting a polarising filter only light in one plane is transmitted. A second polarising filter is oriented at right angles to the first, and the model placed between them. Since the two filters are at right angles, no light is transmitted when the model is unstressed. When the model is stressed, coloured fringes appear which connect points of equal difference between the two principal stresses. The colour gives a clear visual picture, and often make fascinating patterns; the gradual merging of the colours, however, makes a white light source unsuitable for numerical work, and a monochromatic light is used to obtain alternate black and light fringes.

The success of Coker's work in the early 1930's was largely due to the development of photoelastically sensitive materials which could be readily machined into scale models. Celluloid was used initially. Numerous other sheet and casting resins have been used since, *e.g.* Bakelite, Perspex, Catalin and Araldite. Photoelasticity is particularly suitable for showing up stress concentrations, and it has therefore played a prominent part in designing machine parts incorporating notches or sharp corners.

In 1935 Solakian discovered that photoelastic stress patterns could be frozen in certain phenolformaldehyde plastics by stressing them at 75°C, and cooling them at room temperature while still under load. Internal stress patterns can therefore be obtained by cutting the solid model into slices which are then analyzed in a photoelastic bench. The method has, however, found no significant architectural application.

More important to our purpose are the photoelastic coating techniques developed by Zandman in the 1950's [2.23]. Reflected photoelastic fringes can be obtained by coating the model with a thin sheet of photo-elastic material, which is backed by a reflective adhesive or else by a reflecting model surface. The reflective technique is not as sensitive as the conventional transmission method; but it can be used on curved surfaces, such as shells [2.24].

Like the previous methods, photoelasticity requires models to be directly loaded, but yields the strains only indirectly. Conversion of the fringes into data useful for structural design, by graphical methods or by calculation, is an operation which may require more effort than the model test.

2.8. Direct Model Analysis

All the methods of model analysis discussed so far give strains only indirectly; the results obtained must be transformed by graphical or numerical means, and experimental errors can be seriously magnified in the process (see, for example, Fig. 2.5). The Moiré and photoelastic experiments give a direct visual image, but no direct quantitative data. Some cannot be applied in three dimensions at all, others only with difficulty, or over a limited range of solid geometry (e.g. surfaces curved in one direction only).

All structures are, of course, three-dimensional. The majority, however, can be regarded as an assembly of two-dimensional elements, and this greatly simplifies their design. Because of the ease with which liquid concrete can be made to assume a great range of shapes, structures which cannot be broken up into two-dimensional elements have recently become more common. In many concrete structures it is by no means obvious which are the dominating internal forces and moments, which are unimportant, and which exercise significant secondary effects. In unfamiliar shell forms it is difficult to predict whether membrane stresses, which cause deformation only within the shell surface, or bending stresses, will be dominant. We cannot even be certain at all times where the critical stresses in the structure occur.

Direct methods of structural model analysis are less likely to produce very large errors, because the intermediate stages between the measurement and the final result are fewer. The measurement can be seriously in error if the strains measured are below the accuracy of the strain measuring device, but we know when this happens.

Direct model analysis can, as a preliminary design tool, give a rapid approximate analysis. In the case of Le Corbusier's design for the Philips Pavilion at the Brussels International Fair, a complex hyperbolic paraboloid in prestressed concrete, Bouma tested a plaster model in one week to prove the feasibility of the concept [2.43].

2.9. Elasticity versus Ultimate Strength

Structural design has for more than a century been based mainly on the elastic theory (*see* Section 2.1), which uses two criteria. One is the condition that forces anywhere must balance for *equilibrium*, which can be expressed in terms of stresses. The other condition requires the change in geometry (*i.e.* the elastic deformation of the structure) to be the same, or *compatible*, in two adjoining structural members at their point of contact, and this can be expressed in terms of strains.

In experimental stress analysis it is possible to measure strains and forces, but not stresses. The limiting criterion, however, is normally a stress criterion. We assume that the limiting load is reached when the stress anywhere within the structure reaches the maximum safe elastic stress, or working stress. The directness of a method of model analysis based on strain measurement therefore depends on the proportionality of stress and strain.

If we consider an element, say a small unit cube, of a material, the principal strain in the *x*-direction

$$\varepsilon_x = \frac{\sigma_x - \mu\sigma_y - \mu\sigma_z}{E}$$

where σ_x, σ_y and σ_z are the principal stresses along three perpendicular axes, E is the modulus of elasticity, and μ is Poisson's ratio. (The equations relating stresses and strains are given in most books on the Strength of Materials, *e.g.* 2.26.)

Strain measurements can be translated directly into stresses if Poisson's ratio is nil, and if we know the modulus of elasticity. Poisson's ratio ranges from 0 to $\frac{1}{2}$, the latter for fully plastic materials (*i.e.* plastic in the mechanical sense, like steel at the yield point). For model concrete it is about 0·15, but even the comparatively high values of some plastics are not serious if the strain gauges are orientated, if necessary by trial and error, in the direction of the highest stresses.

Determination of the exact value of the modulus of elasticity is more difficult, because concrete and most model materials exhibit a good deal of creep (*see* footnote, Section 2.4); the problems created by creep for the interpretation of direct model analysis are discussed in more detail in Section 4.4.

In the 19th century theoretical solutions could only be obtained by working within the linear range of Hooke's Law. In limiting direct model analysis to the elastic range, we are doing no more, and no less, than providing an elastic solution by mechanical means. There is some gain in accuracy, if we are able to reproduce the boundary conditions more precisely, and a loss in accuracy, if the strains are close to the limit of instrumental sensitivity.

Ultimate strength models must be compared with the ultimate strength theory, rather than with elastic solutions. It is more important to know the ultimate strength of a structure than the load at which the elastic working stress is reached, and in the last thirty years ultimate strength solutions have been obtained for a substantial range of problems. Direct model analysis can be used to extend this range; for example, there are at present no satisfactory theoretical solutions for the ultimate strength of shells; but the technique of testing shell models to failure is now well established.

It is desirable to have information on both the elastic deformation of the structure and on its ultimate strength. While it is very rare to perform both the elastic and ultimate strength calculations, it is normal practice to make strain measurements on an ultimate strength model.

Unlike most indirect methods, direct model analysis can easily be extended to failure if the model material is chosen to have a similar stress–strain curve to the material of the prototype. It is difficult, however, to meet this requirement, except by using the same material. Some of the advantages resulting from a free choice of model materials, such as ease in making the model to accurate dimensions and large elastic strains, are then lost.

2.10. Brittle Coatings

The idea of examining surface strains by observing the cracking of a brittle coating goes back to the earliest days of material testing. The characteristic cracking of mill scale on a piece of hot-rolled steel during a test to destruction must have been observed at quite an early date. It is a simple matter to show up plastic strains in steel structures by coating the surface with shellac, or even with chalk.

By noting the appearance of the cracks, the magnitude and direction of the principal tensile strains are obtained directly. Compressive strains can be determined by applying a coating when the test piece is under load, and releasing it after the coating has dried.

Unfortunately few brittle coatings crack at strains within the elastic range of steel, concrete and aluminium. The Magnaflux Corporation of America has produced a material *Stresscoat* which cracks at a tensile strain of about $7-8 \times 10^{-3}$; but even this is a rather high strain. The material is expensive and poisonous, so that special precautions are needed.

In spite of the directness of the technique and the ease with which it can be used on three-dimensional models, it has so far produced no methods for the design of architectural structures which could not be achieved more readily by other methods.

2.11. Elastic Models Instrumented with Strain Gauges

While three-dimensional scale models have been used in the design of dams for many years, the technique has only recently come into prominence for architectural structures.

Oberti used lightweight mechanical extensometers on an elastic model (Fig. 2.9) of Nervi's first large aircraft hangar in 1935 [2.27]. Torroja had used a small scale model in the previous year for the design of an operating theatre in the Madrid University Hospital, but apparently without detailed strain measurements [2.28].

The invention of electric resistance strain gauges in the late 1930's and the experience gained in their use in aircraft research during the 1939–45 war, greatly extended the potential of direct model analysis. A much larger number of gauge points could now be used, and readings taken from a central control point. The cost of providing and fixing a large number of gauges is still a problem. The recent improvement in accuracy and reduction in size of demountable strain gauges, however, has made it possible to conduct at least a preliminary strain survey on a model with a single demountable strain gauge.

In the late 1940's and in the 1950's a number of laboratories started to make extensive strain measurements of three-dimensional models of architectural structures [2.29 to 2.36]. A comprehensive bibliography of work prior to 1957 has been given by one of the authors [2.37]. Since then the literature on direct model analysis has increased considerably, and it is listed quarterly in the *Magazine of Concrete Research*. In direct model analysis, technique is more important than in indirect analysis because there is a variety of model materials and strain-gauging methods, each having advantages and limitations, and it is necessary to assess their relevance to any particular problem (*see* Section 4.4).

Fig. 2.9. Structural model of the Orvieto hangar tested at the Model Testing Laboratory of the Milan Polytechnic Institute by Oberti in 1935 [2.27]. The model was made from celluloid, and strains were measured with Huggenberger tensometers.

The principal requirements for the material of an elastic model are ease of manufacture and high elastic deformation. Plastics of relatively low strength, but also with a low modulus of elasticity are preferable to stronger materials, because they produce larger elastic strains. A low modulus of elasticity reduces the model load (*see* Section 3.16), and this simplifies the design of the equipment. The acrylic plastics (*Perspex, Plexiglas, Lucite*) have been frequently used because they are readily available in sheets and rods, they can easily be welded into complex space frames [2.38] or moulded at a moderate temperature [2.36]. The main disadvantage of thermoplastic materials is their high rate of creep.

Casting resins, or thermosetting plastics, exhibit little creep, and are useful for moulding complex shapes; because of their high shrinkage dimensional accuracy is not always possible.

Plaster and concrete are used more particularly when the ultimate strength of the model is required in addition to its elastic behaviour.

2.12. Ultimate Strength Models

Direct models can be carried beyond the ultimate strength to failure provided the similarity is not limited to the dimensions, but also extends to the stress–strain diagram of the material. This is achieved when the same material is used in the model and in the prototype.

Ultimate strength modelling of steel structures thus presents no material problems, although the copying of steel sections on the model scale limits its scope [2.39].

Most ultimate strength models have been made for concrete structures. Care has to be taken in scaling down the aggregate and the reinforcement to model size. Small-diameter steel wires often have different properties from full-size bars (*see Section* 4.4).

For certain problems the model is designed purely for the determination of the ultimate strength. Models of brick and masonry structures were already tested in the 18th century (*e.g.* the work of Danizy of voussoir arches, ref. 2.2, p. 19). Because masonry structures are still not amenable to theoretical analysis, there has recently been a renewed interest in the model approach [2.40].

Another fruitful field for model analysis is the buckling failure of elastic materials [2.41] (*see* Fig. 2.10), and of "brittle" struts formed by an assembly of blocks [2.42].

2.13. Mechanical Analogues

It is sometimes difficult to draw the boundary between mechanical analogues and indirect models, nor is the distinction important in

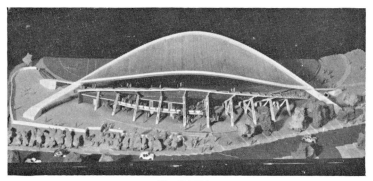

Fig. 2.10(a).

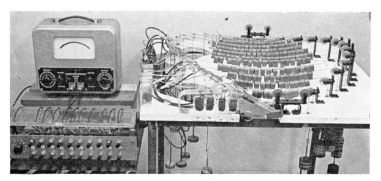

Fig. 2.10(b).

Fig. 2.10(c).

Fig. 2.10(d).

Fig. 2.10(e).

Fig. 2.10.   Buckling of the arch of a suspension structure. (Architectural Science Laboratory, University of Sydney.) (a) Architectural model, (b) structural model, (c), (d), (e) three modes of elastic buckling; the deformation is fully recovered on unloading.

practice. There are many different analogues (B 10, also B 1 and 2), and their usefulness is frequently limited to a specific problem. At one time they were widely used for the numerical solution of problems. The first cost of the equipment may prove excessive, however, unless it is in continuing use, since many of the mathematical equations, for which analogues have been set up, can today be solved readily with a digital computer.

Mechanical analogues for structural problems are too numerous to mention in this section, and the torsion analogue may serve as an example. Prandtl observed in 1903 that the equation of the elastic torsion function and the equation for the transverse deformation of a stretched membrane are similar [2.44].

Elastic Torsion	*Membrane*

$$\frac{\partial^2 \phi}{\partial x^2} + \frac{\partial^2 \phi}{\partial y^2} = -\frac{2G\tau}{l} \qquad\qquad \frac{\partial^2 z}{\partial x^2} + \frac{\partial^2 z}{\partial y^2} = -\frac{p}{T}$$

where ϕ is the elastic torsion function, x, y are the co-ordinates of cross-section, G is the torsion modulus of elasticity, and τ/l is the angle of twist per unit length.

where z is the transverse deflection of the membrane, x, y are the co-ordinates of the membrane base, p is the pressure acting on the membrane, and T is the surface tension in the membrane.

The two equations have the same structure, and the stress function within the cross-section may be determined by measuring the deflection of the membrane, provided the boundary conditions are the same. This requires that:

(i) the boundary of the membrane is the same shape as the boundary of the cross-section of the torsion section, *i.e.* the membrane is stretched over a hole of the shape of cross-section;

(ii) along the boundary $\phi = 0$, so that $z = 0$. This means that the membrane must have zero deflection at the edge of the hole, *i.e.* touch the edge.

The shear stresses are the differential coefficients of ϕ, *i.e.* the slope of the membrane at the corresponding point. The torsional resistance moment is the integral of ϕ, corresponding to the volume displaced by the membrane. Since St. Venant's solution of the torsion problem was limited to a few regular sections, the apparatus (Fig. 2.11) has been used to obtain the torsion constants for irregular shapes, such as structural steel sections. The membrane shape can be obtained easily by cutting an appropriate hole in a box, fixing a thin sheet of rubber over it, and using a bicycle pump to apply the pressure. Measuring the contours of the membrane, however, is laborious.

Another analogue was devised by Nadai in 1923 for plastic torsion, *i.e.* the ultimate load condition in a perfectly plastic material when the shear stress becomes uniform over the entire section [2.45]. A heap of sand settles at a constant slope, the angle of repose of the sand grains corresponding to the constant shear stress. The function of a sand heap, piled on a piece cut from the cross-section, and the plastic torsion function are therefore similar.

Plastic torsion	*Sand heap*
$$\left(\frac{\partial \Psi}{\partial x}\right)^2 + \left(\frac{\partial \Psi}{\partial y}\right)^2 = v^2$$	$$\left(\frac{\partial z}{\partial x}\right)^2 + \left(\frac{\partial z}{\partial y}\right)^2 = m^2$$
where Ψ is the plastic torsion function, x, y are the co-ordinates of cross-section, and v is the constant magnitude of shear stress throughout cross-section.	where z is the height of sand heap, x, y are the co-ordinates of the base of the sand heap, and m is the constant slope of the sand heap.

The magnitude of the shear stress is constant in perfectly plastic torsion, corresponding to the uniform slope of the sand heap. The torsional resistance moment is the integral of Ψ, corresponding to the volume of sand. The *experiment* is easily performed (Fig. 2.12), and the equipment can be calibrated by first piling sand over a simple cross-section (circle or rectangle), and then using the same sand over the cross-section under investigation. The weight of sand over the first cross-section of known torsional strength serves as a calibration for the second section. The *calculation* of the plastic torsional resistance on the other hand is also simple, since it requires only the calculation of the volume contained under a "roof" of constant slope over the cross-section.

By a combination of Prandtl's and Nadai's analogues it is possible to deduce an analogue for elasto–plastic torsion. We start with the membrane analogue, *i.e.* a box with a hole equal to the cross-section, fitted with a membrane. We place over this hole a transparent roof, which has the shape of the appropriate sandheap. When the membrane is pumped up, it will eventually touch the roof,

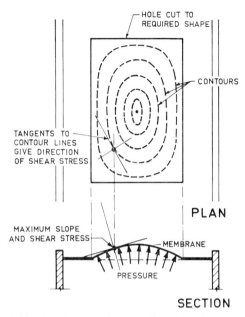

Fig. 2.11. Prandtl's membrane analogue for elastic torsion.

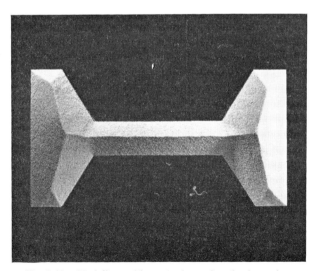

Fig. 2.12. Nadai's sand-heap analogue for plastic torsion.

and be stopped by it, indicating that the material has reached the plastic shear stress (Fig. 2.13). As the pressure is increased, the area of contact between the membrane and the roof is increased, and this shows the progress of plastic stress distribution with load. If the membrane is coated with liquid, dust, or grease, the clarity of the image is improved. This elasto–plastic model is helpful in showing the points of weakness in the section, and consequently the best way of arranging the reinforcement, say for concrete. If no quantitative results are required, very simple equipment suffices. The mathematical solution of the elasto–plastic torsion problem is laborious for all but very simple sections, because it involves a discontinuity between a second-order and a second-degree partial differential equation.

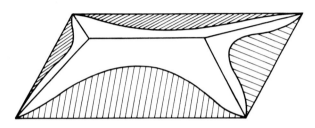

Fig. 2.13. Analogue for elasto–plastic torsion. The portions of contact between the blown-up membrane and the transparent roof above it are the plastic zones of the cross-section.

2.14. Electrical Analogues

There is an even wider range of electrical analogues for the solution of structural problems (B 10, B 1, B 2). Most electrical analogues are assembled from standard components, such as resistances, capacitors, switches and galvanometers. The cost of a new analogue may consist largely of labour, since the parts are often available.

Bush [2.47] has shown the similarity between the equilibrium at a joint and Kirchhoff's Current Law, and then extended it to the slope–deflection equations.

Slope	*Current*
$$M = \frac{\theta}{EI/l}$$	$$I = \frac{V}{R}$$
where M is the bending moment, θ is the slope, E is the modulus of elasticity, I is the second moment of area, and l is the length.	where I is the current, V is the voltage, and R is the resistance.
Slope–deflection equation	*Bush equation*
$$M_{AB} = M'_{AB} - \frac{2EI}{l}(2\theta_A + \theta_B)$$	$$I_{AB} = I'_{AB} - \frac{1}{R}(2V_A - V_B)$$

where A and B have the significance shown in Fig. 2.14, and M' is the fixed-end moment.

This equation has been used in a number of analysers, of which Bray's [2.46] may serve as an example. Fig. 2.15 shows the circuit for a two-span continuous beam, and its bending moment diagram.

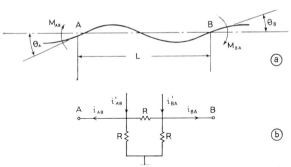

Fig. 2.14. Bush's electrical analogue for the slope–deflection equation. (a) The slope–deflection equation, (b) the analogous electrical circuit. (*After Bray* [2.46]).

If the analyser was limited to continuous beams and rectangular frames without side-sway, it would offer no advantages over moment-distribution calculations. Solutions of frames subject to sway are sometimes tedious by moment distribution because of slow convergence. The Bray analyser uses auxiliary shear circuits to allow for displacements. These can be used to introduce side-sway, sinking support, or thermal movement.

Side-sway equation

$$M_{AB} = M'_{AB} - \frac{2EI}{l}\left(2\theta_A + \theta_B + 3\frac{\Delta}{L}\right)$$

where Δ is the relative lateral displacement of the end of the member due to side-sway (or a sinking support or thermal expansion or contraction).

Bray equation

$$I_{AB} = I'_{AB} - \frac{1}{R}\left(2V_A - V_B - v\right)$$

where v is the terminal voltage of the auxiliary circuit.

Another group of analogues is based on Castigliano's method of minimizing the strain-energy stored in the member. This is modelled by a circuit in which the current, arranged to minimize the electrical

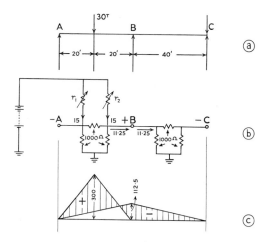

Fig. 2.15. Bray's electrical-analyser circuit for a two-span continuous beam [2.46]. (a) Loads and dimensions, (b) the analogous electrical circuit; the current at **B** is measured by inserting a meter, (c) bending moment diagram; the fixing moment at **B** is obtained from the electrical analogue. The statically determinate bending moments are drawn in the usual way.

power, corresponds to a reaction which minimizes the strain-energy; the voltage corresponds to the deformation of the frame. This technique, proposed by Ryder in 1953 [2.48] has been used for analogue computers in the U.S.A. and in Australasia.

It is doubtful, however, whether it would be worthwhile to build an electrical analogue for rigid frames today, when programs for the solution of rigid frames by digital computer are readily available.

Chapter 3

Principles of Dimensional Theory and Similarity

3.1. Historical Background

As mentioned in Section 2.1 [2.1], Galileo, in the beginning of the 17th century, discoursed, among other things, on the notion of physical similarity with the utmost clarity and drew illustrations from structures living and dead.

There was, and still is, a tendency to regard a geometrically true replica of a structure to be just as structurally adequate as the original. That is to say, that geometrical similarity results in structural similarity; this, however, is a fallacy.

Galileo studied the relationship between the flexural strength of geometrically similar cantilevered and simply supported beams and exposed this fallacy by giving a valid explanation of the "weakness of giants". For the beams he concluded that the bending moments due to self weight vary as the fourth power of the geometric scale factor, whereas the resisting moments vary only as the third power. Therefore as the replica is made increasingly large whilst the strength and specific weight of the material remains constant, a point may be reached at which the applied moments outstrip the resisting moments by an amount equal to the initial margin of safety. When this occurs, the "giant" beam fails.

Galileo presented two possible solutions to this problem; either the material strength must be increased, or the specific weight of the material decreased. Their length (l) may be combined with the strength (σ) and specific weight (γ) to give the dimensionless product (*see* Section 3.9) $l\gamma/\sigma$.

In modern terminology, physical similarity will be obtained if this product $l\gamma/\sigma$ has the same value for both the prototype and its model. It therefore is a vital scale factor in the choice of suitable materials for modelling such structures as dams where self weight and other gravity forces play an essential part. It is most appropriate that this dimensionless product, or number, be called the *Galileo Number* [3.1] in honour of Galileo who first formulated it.

Darcy Wentworth Thompson [3.2] in *On Growth and Form* also discussed the problem of the "weakness of giants", and cited the biological fact that "as the size of an animal increases, the limbs tend to become thicker and shorter and the whole skeleton bulkier and heavier". Thus bones made up some 8% of the body of mouse, 13 or 14% of dog and 17 or 18% of the body of a man. However, skeletal proportions differ little in a porpoise and a whale because the critical influence of self weight has been almost negated by the effects of buoyancy.

In architecture the transition from the heavy and closely spaced columns of Greek Temples through the moderate proportions of reinforced concrete structures to the slenderness of structural steel frames has been accomplished principally by the manifold up-grading of the strength of the respective material of construction.

3.2. The Experimental Approach

In view of Galileo's preoccupation with scientific experimentation, it is not surprising that he pioneered the theory of similitude. His blend of theoretical insight and experimental verification is still, after more than three centuries, the method of contemporary science and technology.

The scientific approach to problems may be considered to comprise the successive stages of recognition, definition, compilation, analysis, synthesis and evaluation. Fig. 3.1 is a simplified flow diagram illustrating this scientific process. Analytical reasoning and conjecture play important parts throughout the process but experimental research is often vital to a meaningful compilation of data and the sensible evaluation of hypotheses.

We put forward here the thesis that this scientific approach is directly applicable to the problems of architecture. Its appropriateness to some problems readily amenable to quantitative analytical consideration (*e.g.* structural design) is accepted, but its extension to the more qualitative aspects of architectural design (*e.g.* visual judgment) is only at its infancy. Nevertheless, a more systematic and rational approach to solving architectural problems is lacking, and thinking scientifically may provide a more satisfactory convergence rate in the design process.

This book is devoted to a discussion and presentation of the experimental methods and tools relevant to architecture, and it must be considered in the wider context of the scientific approach. In this chapter we discuss the principles of dimensional analysis and similarity pioneered by Galileo, and developed by later scientists and engineers to become the basis for model design and interpretation.

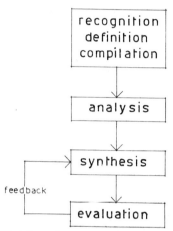

Fig. 3.1. Simplified flow diagram of the scientific process. The first stage is always recognition and definition of the problem and the compilation of available data. This is followed by analysis, synthesis and then evaluation. Of particular importance is the feedback from evaluation to synthesis.

3.3. Units and Dimensions

Physical observations possess two general characteristics; qualitative and quantitative. Thus a characteristic may be distinguished by its qualitative nature or *dimension*, whereas its extent or degree of occurrence may be denoted by a *unit* of measure. For example, a linear characteristic is said to have a dimension of length, which can be measured in inches. The dimension does not change provided the characteristic is a linear one, but the number of units it represents depends on the size of the particular unit of measure adopted.

In a discussion of units and dimensions it is important to consider three aspects:

(i)   the size of the unit,
(ii) the operational procedure for the use of this unit, and
(iii) the datum from which measurements are made.

Thus, a full description of a length of 6 inches is that it has a length dimension, a unit size of 1 inch, a measuring procedure using a ruler and the measurements begin at zero datum.

Mechanical quantities can be described in terms of three basic dimensions, namely, mass, length and time. With thermal problems an additional dimension is ascribed to temperature and, under certain conditions, a dimension is also given to heat. The choice of a basic set of dimensions is not absolute, but depends on the nature of the problem and the operational procedure adopted for measurement. Thus a linear measure is customary and convenient, but we are at liberty to forsake the ruler and adopt a technique of measuring areas directly. This renders area more basic than length, although it is likely to be less convenient. Similarly it is sometimes possible to replace temperature scales by colour measurements.

A simple and useful application of the dimensional concept is in the conversion from one system of units to another. As an illustration, let us consider a velocity of 60 miles per hour and express it in terms of feet per second.

Since 1 mile = 5,280 feet and 1 hour = 3,600 seconds:

$$60 \left[\frac{\text{mile}}{\text{hour}} \right] = 60 \left[\frac{5,280 \text{ feet}}{3,600 \text{ seconds}} \right] = 88 \text{ feet per second.}$$

Thus conversion is accomplished by substituting the numerical factors between the respective units.

3.4. Dimensional Homogeneity

In the theory of dimensional analysis the principle of dimensional homogeneity between the physical quantities appearing in an equation is of fundamental importance. Its validity is regarded here as axiomatic.

Absolute numerical equality of quantities is obtained only when these quantities are similar dimensionally. More generally, because it can be shown [3.3] that the dimension of any quantity may be expressed in terms of some exponential combination of the basic set, there must be equality in the corresponding exponents appearing in the dimensions of all additive terms of an equation. Thus, if the dimensions of physical quantities appearing on each side of an equation are $M^a L^b T^c$ and $M^\alpha L^\beta T^\gamma$, respectively, then dimensional homogeneity demands the equality of the corresponding exponents such that $a = \alpha$, $b = \beta$ and $c = \gamma$. Furthermore, it can be shown that an equation of the form

$$x = m + n + o + \ldots + t$$

is dimensionally homogeneous if, and only if, the variables x, m, n, $o \ldots t$, all have the same dimension.

Two useful applications of the principle of dimensional homogeneity will be considered in the next two sections:

    (i)   checking the general validity of an equation, and
    (ii) developing the form of an equation.

3.5. Checking the General Validity of an Equation

EXAMPLE 3.1. *In the theory of beam design, the moment of resistance M of the beam section is given by the product of the permissible bending stress σ and the modulus of section Z. In another application it is stated that M = 1,500 Z.*

It is convenient to adopt force and length as basic dimensions, *i.e.* F and L.

Therefore equation $M = \sigma Z$ takes the dimensional form

$$[FL] = [FL^{-2}][L^3]$$
$$= [FL]$$

which shows dimensional homogeneity.

Similarly, the equation $M = 1,500 Z$ takes the dimensional form

$$[FL] = [L^3]$$

which is dimensionally non-homogeneous.

In this example $M = \sigma Z$ is dimensionally homogeneous and its validity does not depend on the system of units employed, *i.e.* it is completely general. In contrast, the second equation is non-homogeneous which implies that the constant 1,500 is not a pure number but must necessarily carry the dimension of $[FL^{-2}]$ or stress. Therefore, the validity of this equation is *restricted* to the case where the units of permissible bending stress σ are lb/sq in.

EXAMPLE 3.2. *Investigate the generality of the formula* $\sigma = \dfrac{P}{A} \pm \dfrac{M}{Z}$ *used in the solution of elastic stresses in short compression members,* where P is the axial force, A is the area of cross section, M is the bending moment, Z is the modulus of section, and σ is the resultant stress.

Again it is convenient to adopt force and length as basic dimensions, in terms of which the dimensional form of the equation is

$$[FL^{-2}] = \left[\frac{F}{L^2}\right] \pm \left[\frac{FL}{L^3}\right]$$

$$= [FL^{-2}] \pm [FL^{-2}].$$

Thus, every term in the relationship has the same dimension and the given equation is dimensionally homogeneous. It is therefore valid for any consistent system of units.

Choice of Basic Dimensions. Should mass M, length L and time T be preferred, the dimensional equation becomes, bearing in mind that $[F] = [MLT^{-2}]$:

$$[ML^{-1}T^{-2}] = \left[\frac{MLT^2}{L^2}\right] \pm \left[\frac{ML^2T^{-2}}{L^3}\right]$$

$$= [ML^{-1}T^{-2}] \pm [ML^{-1}T^{-2}]$$

which again verifies the generality of the given equation.

3.6. *Developing the Form of an Equation*

The procedure available for the derivation of simple equations is illustrated in this section. The more vital question of determining the significant variables is discussed in example 3.6.

EXAMPLE 3.3. *A simple pendulum consists of a weightless string of length l at the extremity of which is suspended a mass m. Derive an expression for the period, t, if it is assumed that the significant variables of this system are l, m and g (acceleration due to gravity).*

Initially write relationship in the form

$$t = C \, l^a \, m^b \, g^c$$

where C is a constant of proportionality, and a, b and c are unknown exponents. Using basic dimensions M, L and T, the dimensional form of this equation becomes

$$[T] = [L]^a \, [M]^b \, [LT^{-2}]^c.$$

Comparing dimensions on each side we have:

$$\text{mass: } 0 = b$$
$$\text{length: } 0 = a + c$$
$$\text{time: } 1 = -2c.$$

This set of three auxiliary equations may be solved for a, b and c giving

$$b = 0$$
$$c = -\tfrac{1}{2}$$
$$a = +\tfrac{1}{2}$$

Hence the pendulum equation becomes

$$t = C \, l^{\frac{1}{2}} \, m^0 \, g^{-\frac{1}{2}}$$

$$\text{or } t = C \, \sqrt{l/g},$$

which is the required equation.

It is interesting to note that the mass variable is not significant, which is not immediately obvious. The numerical constant can now be determined by performing one series of experiments involving the measurement of t for a number of values of $l\sqrt{/g}$. These values yield a straight line graph whose slope is C.

EXAMPLE 3.4. *A student sets out to derive the equation for the vertical deflection at the free end of a cantilever of rectangular cross section. He conducts four series of experiments, each time varying only one of the four variables, width b and depth d of section, point load W at free end, and span l.*

The experiments yield the following relationships:

$$\text{deflection } y \propto b^{-1}$$
$$\propto d^{-3}$$
$$\propto W$$
$$\propto l^{3}.$$

He therefore concludes that

$$y = C\,W\,l^3\,b^{-1}\,d^{-3}$$

where C is a constant of proportionality.

In a dimensional check, he finds that the dimensions of

left hand side $= [L]$, and

right hand side $= [F]\,[L^3]\,[L^{-1}]\,[L^{-3}]$.

Hence the equation derived is restricted both in the system of units employed and the material of the test beams.

As the theoretical result is $\frac{1}{3}(WL^3/EI)$ or $4(WL^3/Ebd^3)$ it can be seen that the student has omitted consideration of E, the Young's modulus of elasticity. Realising this, he conducts another experiment employing several beams of equal dimensions, but made with different elastic materials, and finds an inverse proportionality between deflection and modulus of elasticity.

The amended equation is then

$$y = k\frac{Wl^3}{Ebd^3}$$

which is dimensionally homogeneous and therefore is the correct formula sought.

3.7. Reduction of Variables

The usefulness of the dimensional concept has been illustrated in Sections 3.3, 3.5 and 3.6 when dealing with unit conversions, checking equations and developing simple relationships. However, another important application of dimensional theory is in the reduction of the number of variables or parameters in order to achieve an economy of experimental effort.

Recalling the beam deflection problem in the previous section, it is seen that the student found it necessary to conduct five different series of experiments, one for each of the variables b, d, W, l and E. If each series required, say, six experiments in order to establish the relationships with a reasonable degree of confidence, a total of thirty experiments would have to be prepared for and conducted. The time and effort is enormous, and yet the problem cannot be be regarded as difficult.

Therefore any means of condensing the problem is worthwhile. This is accomplished by organizing variables to form dimensionless products, generalized by the π-theorem.

3.8. Non-Dimensional Quantities

A non-dimensional quantity is a quantity, physical constant, or any group formed in such a manner that all of the dimensions (and units) cancel identically; it is also called a dimensionless number or product.

If the dimensional equation of a quantity $q = M^a L^b T^c$, then q is non-dimensional if $a = b = c = 0$, or $q = [M^0 L^0 T^0] = [1]$ where [1] denotes zero dimension.

Non-dimensional quantities perform a central role in the theory of dimensional analysis.

EXAMPLE 3.5. *Form a non-dimensional product out of the three quantities E, W and l where*

$$E, \text{Young's modulus} = [FL^{-2}]$$
$$W, \text{force} = [F]$$
$$l, \text{length} = [L].$$

Product $q = E^a W^b L^c$
or, dimensionally, $[1] = [FL^{-2}]^a [F]^b [L]^c$.

Comparing corresponding exponents yields two auxiliary equations in the three exponents:

$$0 = a + b$$
$$0 = -2a + c,$$

whence $$a = + \tfrac{1}{2}c$$
$$b = - \tfrac{1}{2}c$$

where c remains undetermined.

Therefore

$$q = E^{\frac{c}{2}} \, W^{-\frac{c}{2}} \, L^c$$
$$= (EL^2/W)^{\frac{c}{2}}.$$

Removal of the overall exponent by taking the $\frac{c}{2}$th root of both sides yields the dimensionless product in its simplest form, viz. (EL^2/W).

3.9. Primary and Derived Quantities

A *primary* quantity can be written in terms of the first power of one unit of measure according to the specified operational measuring procedure. It should not require the use of two measuring procedures, and it should not require an expression involving any power of the dimension needed other than one. Thus, if the operational procedure is one of length scaling (by tape measure, say) then length is a primary quantity since its dimension is merely L. The area-measure of a plane shape is not a primary quantity as it involves the product of two length measurements, that is, it has dimension L^2, and it is called a *derived* or secondary quantity.

However, should the planimeter replace the tape as a basic operational measure, then it is justifiable to call area, whose dimension is now A, a primary quantity. A length now becomes a derived quantity with the dimension $[A^{\frac{1}{2}}]$. We conclude that there are no absolute fundamental dimensions as the choice is, in fact, the investigator's when he specifies the operational measures.

If mass is regarded as a primary dimension, then force is a derived quantity with dimension $[MLT^{-2}]$.

However, if force is regarded as a primary dimension, then mass is a derived quantity with dimension $[FL^{-1} T^2]$.

In structural model analysis the force, length, time (F, L, T) dimensions system is commonly used as the primary system. It is always possible to express a derived or secondary quantity as a single combination of the powers of the dimensions of the primary quantities. Thus if the primary dimensions are mass [M], length [L], time [T] and temperature [θ], then the dimensions of any secondary quantity q can be shown to be expressible in the form

$$q = M^a L^b T^c \theta^d$$

and the exponents a, b, c and d are constants which may take any real finite values including zero. This possibility has been assumed in the earlier sections of this chapter.

Although temperature is often considered a primary dimension by virtue of its independent operational measure, it may also be derived from the mechanical equivalent of heat if mechanical–heat energy transformation is present in the problem. For example, it is interesting to note that when dealing with microscopic systems, temperature is often expressed in terms of mass, length and time because of the identity of heat with molecular kinetic energy.

3.10. The Buckingham π-theorem

In 1899 Lord Rayleigh employed the theory of dimensional analysis to study the effect of temperature on the viscosity of the gas argon. Fourteen years later, Buckingham [3.4] published the π-theorem without giving a rigorous proof.* The π-theorem is discussed here without proof and interested readers may refer to Langhaar [3.3] for an algebraic proof or to Corrsin [3.5] for a geometrical proof.

Theorem. When a mathematical relationship exists among r physical parameters, and when all these parameters can be expressed in terms of n independent primary dimensions, the relationship can be expressed in terms of $(r-n)$ dimensionless (π) products of the system parameters.

Thus the functional relationship between the r-parameters of a physical system can be written as

$$F_1 (x_1, x_2, x_3 \ldots x_r) = 0 \tag{3.1}$$

where x_1, x_2 . . . x_r are the parameters and F_1 a dimensionally homogeneous function, known or unknown.

---

* The π-theorem is usually attributed to Buckingham, but like most achievements of science its foundations were laid by many other contributors including Fourier, Riabouchinsky and Rayleigh.

The π-theorem asserts that the equivalent relationship is given by

$$F_2 (\pi_1, \pi_2, \pi_3 \ldots \pi_{r-n}) = 0 \qquad (3.2)$$

where F_2 is again a dimensionally homogeneous function, known or unknown, and the π-terms are the dimensionless products.

The rationale of the π-theorem may be established without the use of higher mathematics. Recall what has been accepted, namely,

(i)   that there must be a functional relationship among the r-parameters,
(ii) that this relationship must be dimensionally homogeneous to be meaningful in physical terms,
(iii) that each additive term in the eqn. (3.1) has the same dimensions (consequences of (ii)), and
(iv) that the dimensions of the system parameters can be made up by suitable products of powers of the n independent primary dimensions.

Point (i) justifies the form of eqn. (3.1). This equation may be rewritten, theoretically, as

$$(\text{Term})_1 + (\text{Term})_2 + \ldots = 0$$

where $(\text{Term})_1$ etc. are additive terms if eqn. (3.1) were made explicit. Also by point (iii) the dimension of $(\text{Term})_1$ is $d_1^a d_2^b \ldots d_n^t$ where $d_1, d_2 \ldots d_n$ are the n independent primary dimensions.

Hence n additional terms arise out of the equality of dimensions of the additive terms, giving a total of $(1 + n)$ equations in r-parameters for the system. The extra n equations can be used to eliminate n quantities in the original eqn. (3.1), thus leaving one relationship in $(r - n)$ parameter groups as stated in eqn. (3.2).

Each π-term is made up of n repeating parameters which involve all the dimensions being considered, without forming a dimensionless term, and one parameter which is changed from term to term. This one extra parameter allows the formation of the dimensionless product.

π-terms may be multiplied together or divided by each other (or themselves) without altering their functional relationships:

$$F(\pi_1, \pi_2, \pi_3) = (F(\pi_1/\pi_2, \pi_3)) = 0.$$

EXAMPLE 3.6. *Given that deflection y is a function of the applied load W, the span length dimension l, the cross-sectional area dimension A, the moment of inertia I, the modulus of elasticity E and the shear modulus G. Determine the functional relationship between y and the other parameters.*

This may be written generally as

$$F(y, W, A, I, E, G) = 0.$$

Dimensionally,

$$y = \text{L}$$
$$W = \text{F}$$
$$l = \text{L}$$
$$A = \text{L}^2$$
$$I = \text{L}^4$$
$$E = \text{FL}^{-2}$$
$$G = \text{FL}^{-2}.$$

By inspection, $r = 7$ and $n = 2$; thus there will be five π-terms. Choose E and l as the repeating parameters. The π-terms are

$$\pi_1 = y/1$$
$$\pi_2 = W/El^2$$
$$\pi_3 = A/l^2$$
$$\pi_4 = I/l^4$$
$$\pi_5 = G/E$$

i.e. $F(y/l, W/El^2, A/l^2, I/l^4, G/E) = 0.$

Consider the case in which the effects of G and A are negligible as in the determination of the deflection of a beam neglecting shear and axial deformation; the function now becomes

$$F_1(y/l, W/El^2, I/l^4) = 0.$$

Divide π_2 by π_4 and π_4 by itself to get

$$F_1(y/l, Wl^2/EI) = 0.$$
$$y/l = k_1 . Wl^2/EI,$$
$$\text{i.e.} \quad y = k_1 . Wl^3/EI$$

where k is a constant.

Now consider the case in which the effects of G and I are negligible as in the determination of the deflection (shortening) of a column due to axial load; the function now becomes

$$F_2 \left(y/l, \ W/EI^2, \ A/l^2 \right) = 0.$$

Divide π_2 by π_3 and π_3 by itself to get

$$F_2 \left(y/l, \ W/EA \right) = 0,$$

thus
$$y = k_2 . Wl/EA.$$

Similarly, by neglecting I and considering the effects of shear deformation only, the function now becomes

$$F_3 \left(y/l, \ W/EI^2, \ A/l^2, \ G/E \right) = 0.$$

Divide π_2 by π_5 and the resultant by π_3 to get

$$F_3 \left(y/l, \ W/GA \right) = 0,$$

thus
$$y = k_3 . Wl/GA.$$

3.11. Independence of a Set of Primary Dimensions

The notion of independence (algebraically speaking) of the set of n primary dimensions adopted warrants some comment. In his original formulation of the theorem, Buckingham stated that n was the minimum number of primary dimensions required to construct the dimensions of all the parameters $x_1, x_2 \ldots x_r$. In the majority of cases this is satisfactory, because the n dimensions are independent of one another and the π-theorem yields a complete set of π-products [3.6, 3.7].

However, this method of arriving at the number n fails in certain situations as was shown more recently by Van Driest [3.8] and treated with mathematical rigour by Langhaar [3.3]. It is more correct to replace n by k, where k is the largest number of parameters contained in the original list of parameters $x_1, x_2 \ldots x_r$ that will not combine into a non-dimensional form. The value of k is less than or equal to the value of n.

3.12. Similarity and Models

Two phenomena are similar if the characteristics of one can be obtained from the characteristics of the other by a simple conversion, *i.e.* there exist simple scale factors relating the two sets of characteristics. This permits the prediction of the behaviour of one by a knowledge of the behaviour of another. Such systems are termed the *prototype* and *model*, respectively.

To ensure similarity in behaviour, certain conditions governing the choice of the model must be satisfied. These can be deduced from the theory of dimensional analysis as follows.

According to the π-theorem, a system is fully described by the functional relationship

$$F\left(\pi_1, \pi_2 \ldots \pi_{r-n}\right) = 0 \tag{3.2}$$

Any other system possessing an identical functional relationship F among the same $r-n$ π-products of the variables must belong to the same *class* of system. Consequently, a model system must be sought from the same class as the prototype system.

Therefore, selecting a particular member of the class of systems defined by the function F and subscripting it m to denote model, and p to denote prototype, eqn. (3.2) may be written as

$$\left. \begin{array}{l} F\left(\pi_{1p}, \pi_{2p} \ldots \pi_{(r-n)p}\right) = 0 \\ F\left(\pi_{1m}, \pi_{2m} \ldots \pi_{(r-n)m}\right) = 0 \end{array} \right\} \tag{3.3}$$

If the first π-term contains the particular parameter under study, eqn. (3.3) can be modified to the form

$$\pi_{1p} = F_1\left(\pi_{2p}, \pi_{3p} \ldots \pi_{(r-n)p}\right) \tag{3.4}$$

and

$$\pi_{1m} = F_1\left(\pi_{2m}, \pi_{3m} \ldots \pi_{(r-n)m}\right). \tag{3.5}$$

Dividing eqn. (3.4) by eqn. (3.5) gives

$$\frac{\pi_{1p}}{\pi_{1m}} = \frac{F_1\left(\pi_{2p}, \pi_{3p} \ldots \pi_{(r-n)p}\right)}{F_1\left(\pi_{2m}, \pi_{3m} \ldots \pi_{(r-n)m}\right)}. \tag{3.6}$$

Clearly then, if the π-parameters of the function F_1 are identically equal, namely, if

$$\pi_{2p} = \pi_{2m}$$
$$\pi_{3p} = \pi_{3m}$$
$$\pi_{(r-n)p} = \pi_{(r-n)m}$$
$$F_1\left(\pi_{2p}, \pi_{3p} \ldots \pi_{(r-n)p}\right) = F_1\left(\pi_{2m}, \pi_{3m} \ldots \pi_{(r-n)m}\right). \quad (3.7)$$

Hence, from eqn. (3.6),

$$\pi_{1p} = \pi_{1m}. \quad (3.8)$$

Equation (3.8) immediately provides a conversion factor for parameters making up the first π-term. Therefore the two systems satisfy the necessary requirement stated earlier. *Thus the identity of π-products is a necessary and sufficient condition for similarity.*

The ratio of prototype to model variables, e.g., $W_p/W_m = \lambda_w$ is known as *scale ratio*.

EXAMPLE 3.7. *Consider again the deflection problem in Example 3.4. The vertical deflection at the free end of a cantilever depends on four variables; the point load, W, at the free end; the span, l; the moment of inertia of the beam cross-section, I, and the modulus of elasticity of the material, E. Determine the scale ratios for deflection, load and inertia.*

This may be written as

$$F(y, W, l, E) = 0.$$

Dimensionally

$$y = [L]$$
$$W = [F]$$
$$l = [L]$$
$$I = [L^4]$$
$$E = [FL^{-2}].$$

By inspection, $r = 5$ and $n = 2$; thus there will be 3 π-terms. Choose E and l as the repeating variables. The π-terms are

$$\pi_1 = y/l$$
$$\pi_2 = W/El^2$$
$$\pi_3 = I/l^4,$$

i.e. $F(y/l, W/El^2, I/l^4) = 0.$

or
$$y_p/l_p = y_m/l_m$$
$$\lambda_y = \lambda_l.$$

Similarly, $$\frac{W_p}{E_p l_p^{\,2}} = \frac{W_m}{E_m l_m^{\,2}}$$

or $$\lambda_W = \lambda_E \lambda_l^{\,2}$$

and $$\frac{I_p}{l_p^{\,4}} = \frac{I_m}{l_m^{\,4}}$$

or $$\lambda_I = \lambda_l^{\,4}.$$

EXAMPLE 3.8. *What are the similarity requirements of the previous example?*

The necessary and sufficient conditions for similarity are satisfied if

$\lambda_y = \lambda_l$ deformation similarity,
$\lambda_W = \lambda_E \lambda_l^{\,2}$ loading similarity, and
$\lambda_I = \lambda_l^{\,4}$ geometrical similarity,

are all satisfied. It can be seen that once the geometrical scale ratio has been decided, the ratio λ_W can only be varied by altering λ_E.

Thus, once the similarity requirements of the problem have been determined, it is possible to evaluate numerically the scale ratios for any particular model.

EXAMPLE 3.9. *It is proposed to use a geometrically similar model to determine deflections and stresses which has the following proto-type : model ratios*

$$\lambda_l \; 20:1$$
$$\overline{}$$
$$\lambda_E \; 10:1.$$
$$\overline{}$$

Determine the scale ratios for loads, deflections and stresses.

From example 3.7,

$$\lambda_W = \lambda_E \lambda_l^{\,2} = 10 \times (20)^2.$$

Hence $$W_p : W_m = 4,000:1,$$

$$\lambda_y = \lambda_l.$$

Hence $$y_p : y_m = 20:1.$$

We need further dimensional analysis to determine the stress scale ratio,

$$F(\sigma, l, E, W) = 0.$$

Use the π-theorem to get

$$F\left(\frac{\sigma l^2}{W}, \frac{W}{El^2}\right) = 0$$

i.e. $\lambda_\sigma = \lambda_W/\lambda_l^2.$

Hence, $\sigma_p : \sigma_m = 4{,}000/20^2 = 10{:}1.$

Note here that the same result for λ_σ could have been obtained by multiplying the two π-terms together to obtain

$$F(\sigma/E) = 0,$$

therefore, $\lambda_\sigma = \lambda_E = 10{:}1.$

3.13. Limitations of the π-theorem

(i) *Choice of significant parameters.*—The π-theorem can offer no guidance on the significance of the parameters. The choice rests with the investigator who must exercise his judgment, aided by experience and intuition. This remark applies only when the state of knowledge of the phenomenon under study is incomplete, as in research type problems.

For every extraneous parameter included, the number of π-products increases by one, demanding one extra series of experiments to be conducted solely for the purpose of proving its irrelevance. In the design of the model the extra π-product becomes an additional restriction, although the mechanics of the dimensional analysis remain valid. On the other hand, if an omission has inadvertently been made, the analysis may lead to an incomplete or erroneous result, or may reach an impasse.

(ii) *Functional relationship not revealed.*—The simple problems discussed deduce the actual functional relationship. This is exceptional, and possible only for a product function such as $t = C\sqrt{l/g}$. It cannot be expected generally from dimensional analysis.

Recent developments in dimensional theory have been directed towards an approximation theory which can assist in the quest for a partial solution or formulation of the problem.

(*iii*) *Relative importance of π-products.*—The π-theorem alone provides no conditions for neglecting one or more π-terms; *e.g.* in example 3.6 the theorem demands complete geometrical similarity. If it is known that this similarity can be relaxed, a wire model suffices.

3.14. Similarity Derived from Known Formulae

Dimensional analysis approaches a problem with complete generality and does not require knowledge of the physical laws governing the problem. It is used to derive the conditions of similarity; however, in many problems the governing laws are well known, so that they can be used to determine the conditions of similarity.

EXAMPLE 3.10. *Consider a multi-storey frame to be investigated to determine deflection under wind load, and the moments and stresses at the joints of the beams and columns.*

From the formula for flexural deflection

$$y \propto \frac{Wl^3}{EI}$$

thus

$$\lambda_y = \frac{\lambda_W \lambda_l^3}{\lambda_E \lambda_I}.$$

If geometrical similarity for deformations is to be preserved

$$\lambda_y = \lambda_l. \tag{3.9}$$

Therefore the load scale ratio can be written as

$$\lambda_W = \frac{\lambda_E \lambda_I}{\lambda_l^2}. \tag{3.10}$$

Moments can be written as

$$M = W.l$$

so the moment scale ratio is

$$\lambda_M = \lambda_W \lambda_l \qquad (3.11)$$

and substituting for λ_W from eqn. (3.10) into 3.11

$$\lambda_M = \frac{\lambda_E \lambda_I}{\lambda_l}. \qquad (3.12)$$

Stresses can be written as

$$\sigma = M/Z \qquad (3.13)$$

where $Z = I/\frac{1}{2}l$.

Thus, $$\lambda_\sigma = \lambda_M/\lambda_Z. \qquad (3.14)$$

Substituting for λ_M from eqn. (3.12) and for Z in eqn. (3.14)

$$\lambda_\sigma = \frac{\lambda_E \lambda_I}{\lambda_l} \frac{\lambda_l}{\lambda_I}$$

so $$\lambda_\sigma = \lambda_E.$$

The similarity conditions for deflections, moments and stresses have been obtained without recourse to the π-theorem.

3.15. Classes of Similarity

Section 3.12 establishes the necessary and sufficient conditions for the similarity of physical systems. Fig. 3.2 presents the three classes of similarity which furnish the means for solving the proto-type problem.

The prototype behaviour is specified by its parameters. If its governing equation is known from a theoretical analysis, it forms an explicit mathematical representation, or model, of the prototype. If it is amenable to an analytical solution for the given boundary conditions, then a theoretical prediction of the prototype response is obtained. This is a powerful method, particularly since the intro-duction of digital computation.

When the governing equation of the prototype, though known, is not suitable for an analytical solution, a model is used. This must belong to the same class of systems as the prototype, but may be based on either physical or mathematical similarity. For physical similarity, a *physical model* is constructed which has the same governing equation as the prototype. Mathematical similarity can be satisfied either by a *dissimilar or analogous model* (*see* Sections 2.13 and 2.14).

If the governing equation is wholly or partially unknown, only physical similarity can provide a solution; a physical model is then indispensable.

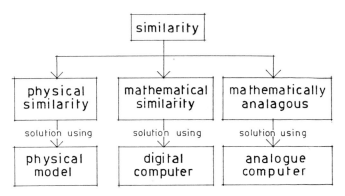

Fig. 3.2. The three classes of similarity—physical, mathematical and mathematically analogous—with the method of obtaining the solution.

At the other extreme end of the similarity scale is the *descriptive model* for specifying a problem not expressible in quantitative terms (*see* Section 6.2).

Perfect similarity is seldom obtainable as it is often necessary to introduce approximations. For example, in order to achieve practical results, approximations may have to be applied in the mathematical formulation and solution of the mathematical model or in the construction, testing and interpretation of a physical model. Instances readily coming to mind are the neglect of shear strain in the ordinary bending theory; relaxation methods for numerical solution of analytical problems; and employing a plastic to model reinforced concrete.

If all similarity conditions are fulfilled a *true model* is produced. Approximate similarity is achieved by *distorted models* which are often quite adequate for their particular tasks. If the degree of distortion is large, extrapolation of model results is prone to uncertain errors, and some auxiliary investigations may then be necessary in order to define the confidence limits and conditions under which results are acceptable [3.9 and 3.10].

3.16. Conditions for Structural Similitude

A list of the significant variables for the general three-dimensional structure is given in Table 3.1, together with the corresponding dimensions and similitude relations. The choice of the variables indicates their significance to the design of the model; thus, self-weight, temperature and dynamic actions are expressed in terms of specific mass, temperature, time and acceleration. The derivation of the latter follow from Buckingham's π-theorem.

Adopting the following four basic dimensions:

mass	M
length	L
time	T
temperature	θ

all the variables may be derived using the π-theorem outlined in Section 3.10.

Table 3.1

Dimensional analysis of a general structure

Variable	Symbol	Dimension	Similitude Condition
Typical length	l	[L]	$l_p = \lambda_l l_m$
Young's Modulus	E	$[ML^{-1}T^{-2}]$	$E_p = \lambda_E E_m$
Poisson's Ratio	μ	[1]	$\mu_p = \mu_m$
Specific Mass	ρ	$[ML^{-3}]$	$\rho_p = \lambda_E \lambda_a^{-1} \lambda_l^{-1} \rho_m$
Coefficient of Expansion	a	$[\theta^{-1}]$	$a_p = \lambda_a a_m$
Temperature	θ	$[\theta]$	$\theta_p = \lambda_a^{-1} \theta_m$
Time	t	[T]	$t_p^2 = \lambda_l \lambda_a^{-1} t_m^2$
Force	P	$[MLT^{-2}]$	$P_p = \lambda_E \lambda_l^2 P_m$
Pressure	p	$[ML^{-1}T^{-2}]$	$p_p = \lambda_E p_m$
Acceleration	a	$[LT^{-2}]$	$a_p = \lambda_a a_m$
Stress	σ	$[ML^{-1}T^{-2}]$	$\sigma_p = \lambda_E \sigma_m$
Strain	ε	[1]	$\varepsilon_p = \varepsilon_m$
Displacement	u	[L]	$u_p = \lambda_l u_m$

From Table 3.1 it can be seen that arbitrarily fixing the four scale ratios λ_1, λ_E, λ_a and λ_a, determines the values of the remaining scale ratios which can be computed from the relevant equations given in the table.

Derived scale factors are deduced from the equations given in Table 3.1.

$$\mu_p = \mu_m \quad \text{or} \quad \lambda_\mu = \frac{\mu_p}{\mu_m} = 1,$$

i.e. Poisson's ratio must be the same for model and prototype.

$$\rho_p = \lambda_E \, \lambda_a^{-1} \, \lambda_l^{-1} \, \rho_m \quad \text{or} \quad \lambda_\rho = \frac{\lambda_E}{\lambda_a \lambda_l}.$$

For body forces due to gravity $\lambda_a = 1$, giving $\lambda_\rho = \lambda_E/\lambda_l$ which is often restrictive in the selection of model scale λ because of the limited range of λ_ρ normally available.

$$\theta_p = \lambda_a^{-1} \, \theta_m \quad \text{or} \quad \lambda_\theta = \frac{\theta_p}{\theta_m} = \frac{1}{\lambda_a},$$

i.e. the temperature scale factor is the inverse of the expansion coefficient scale factor.

$$t_p^2 = \lambda_l \, \lambda_a^{-1} \, t_m^2 \quad \text{or} \quad \lambda_t = \frac{t_p}{t_m} = \sqrt{\lambda_l/\lambda_a},$$

i.e. the time scale factor is a function of those for length and acceleration.

$$P_p = \lambda_E \, \lambda_l^2 \, P_m \quad \text{or} \quad \lambda_p = \frac{P_p}{P_m} = \lambda_E \, \lambda_l^2,$$

$$p_p = \lambda_E \, p_m \quad \text{or} \quad \lambda_p = \frac{p_p}{p_m} = \lambda_E$$

and $$\sigma_p = \lambda_E \, \sigma_m \quad \text{or} \quad \lambda_\sigma = \frac{\sigma_p}{\sigma_m} = \lambda_E,$$

i.e. pressure, stress and elastic modulus scale factors are equal by virtue of their identical dimensions.

$$\varepsilon_p = \varepsilon_m \quad \text{or} \quad \lambda_\varepsilon = \frac{\varepsilon_p}{\varepsilon_m} = 1,$$

i.e. strain levels under homologous loadings are exactly alike.

$$u_p = \lambda_l\, u_m \quad \text{or} \quad \lambda_u = \frac{u_p}{u_m} = \lambda_l,$$

i.e. there is exact geometrical similitude of deformations.

If all the above similarity conditions are to be observed, practical difficulties may arise from the requirements of

$$\lambda_\mu = 1$$

$$\lambda_\rho = \frac{\lambda_E}{\lambda_a\, \lambda_l}$$

$$\lambda_\theta = \frac{1}{\lambda_a}$$

and
$$\lambda_t = \sqrt{\lambda_l/\lambda_a}\ .$$

$\lambda_\mu = 1$. This is seldom exactly satisfied. Some distortion is often justified because of the relatively small errors introduced; this has been analytically proved for a number of problems [3.11].

$\lambda_\rho = \lambda_E/\lambda_a\lambda_l$. This condition is significant for dynamic model studies, *e.g.* in earthquake design, where inertia forces are set up due to seismic vibrations [3.12]. If λ_E and λ_l have been decided, then λ_a may be chosen to satisfy the equality. The required model acceleration is artificially generated; however, for body forces due to gravity, $\lambda_a = 1$, which makes it more difficult to satisfy $\lambda_\rho = \lambda_E/\lambda_l$ without some restrictions on the model scale. This difficulty may be overcome by:

(i) inducing artificial acceleration in the model, *e.g.* using a large centrifuge [3.13], or

(ii) replacing or augmenting the gravity body forces by external force applied inside or on the surface of the model.

$\lambda_\theta = 1/\lambda_a$. When λ_a is large the temperature for the model is greater than for the prototype, with consequent difficulties in conducting experiments and making measurements at a high temperature (*see* Section 3.17).

$\lambda_t = \sqrt{\lambda_l/\lambda_a}$. If λ_t becomes too large, the model time scale is small. This is of significance if periodic effects have to be measured.

3.17. Similitude Conditions for Ultimate Strength

It has been noted in Chapter 2 that ultimate strength models, properly designed, may be used to predict the mode of failure of the prototype structure. The model material should preferably be identical to that of the actual structure. In ultimate strength models the whole stress-strain behaviour of the material is taken into account, thus raising the question of compatibility between the stress–strain relationships for the materials of the model and prototype.

Referring to Fig. 3.3, let curves 1 and 2 represent prototype and model materials, respectively. Recalling the equality of strains, it is evident that the ultimate strains in compression and tension must be identical for both materials. Furthermore, for non-linear stress–strain characteristics, the similitude condition $\sigma_p = \lambda_E \sigma_m$ must be satisfied in respect to all strain levels. Thus curve 2 may be obtained from curve 1 by the transformation

$$\left.\begin{aligned} \sigma_m &= \frac{1}{\lambda_E}\,\sigma_p \\[2ex] \varepsilon_m &= \varepsilon_p. \end{aligned}\right\} \tag{3.15}$$

In practice, the transformation

$$\left.\begin{aligned} \sigma_m &= \frac{1}{\lambda_\sigma}\,\sigma_p \\[2ex] \varepsilon_m &= \frac{1}{\lambda_\varepsilon}\varepsilon_p \end{aligned}\right\} \tag{3.16}$$

(where λ_σ and λ_ε are the stress and strain scale-factors, respectively), is permissible for conditions where the effect of displacements on the state of stress is not significant. Equation (3.16) transforms curve 1 into curve 3.

It is an advantage to use the same material for prototype and model; but if self-weight is significant, the model weight must be augmented by surface loads to yield a realistic λ_ρ. In dynamic model studies this expedient is not acceptable and another material must be chosen whose density and stress–strain relationship give a more accurate λ_ρ [3.12].

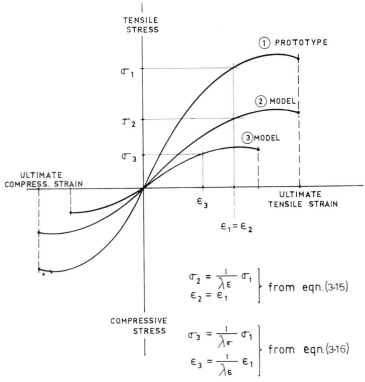

Fig. 3.3. Simulation of non-linear stress–strain curves for ultimate strength models. Curves 1 and 2 represent the prototype and model material stress–strain curve, respectively, when the strains in the prototype and model are the same. In practice, the transformation of curve 1 to curve 3 is possible through stress and strain scale-factors.

3.18. *Similitude Conditions for Temperature Stresses*

Determination of temperature stresses is generally difficult by analytical methods, particularly in concrete structures. An experimental solution has been achieved by Rocha and Serafim [3.14] and Mori [3.15]. Consider the conditions of structural and thermal similitude to be obeyed. The structural similitude conditions have been determined in Section 3.16. For thermal similitude, at the same instant on a time scale, temperatures at corresponding points on the model and the prototype should be proportional. In order to fulfil this condition it suffices to apply, at the surface of the model, temperatures proportional to those that would occur at equivalent points on the surface of the prototype, *i.e.*

$$\theta_p = \lambda_\theta\,\theta_m$$

where
$$\lambda_\theta = \lambda_a^{-1}.$$

Once these conditions are obeyed, the following similitude ratios are obtained for stresses σ, strains ε, displacements u, and time, t:

$$\sigma_p = \lambda_\theta\,\lambda_E\,\lambda_a\,\sigma_m$$
$$\varepsilon_p = \lambda_\theta\,\lambda_a.\varepsilon_m$$
$$u_p = \lambda_\theta.\lambda_l.\lambda_a.u_m$$
$$t_p = \lambda_p.\lambda_l^2.\lambda_c.\lambda_k^{-1}.t_m$$

where $\lambda_c = C_p/C_m$, ratio of specific heats (dimension $[L^2T^{-2}\theta^{-1}]$), and $\lambda_k = k_p/k_m$, ratio of thermal conductivities (dimension $[ML\,T^{-3}\theta^{-1}]$).

3.19. Distorted Models

In some model tests it is desirable to change the scale ratios from those derived by similarity requirements. For example, if the thickness of the model material is constant and a change of inertia is required, only the depth can be varied. This requires a different length scale ratio for depth and thickness.

$$\lambda_I = \lambda_l\,\lambda_d^3.$$

EXAMPLE 3.11. *Investigate the situation when modelling the deflection of a beam whose cross-sectional properties do not comply with the specified length ratio λ_l.*

From example 3.10

$$\lambda_y = \frac{\lambda_W\,\lambda_l^3}{\lambda_E\,\lambda_I}$$
$$\lambda_y = \lambda_l$$
$$\lambda_W = \frac{\lambda_E\,\lambda_I}{\lambda_l^2}. \tag{3 17}$$

It is possible to have $\lambda_I = \lambda_l{}^4$ for deflection similarity provided the load scale ratio is suitably modified. Therefore any cross-sectional shape is acceptable for the model, a fact of practical importance when the prototype beam is of an intricate cross section (Fig. 3.4). Note that the result in eqn. (3.17) was not given by the π-theorem.

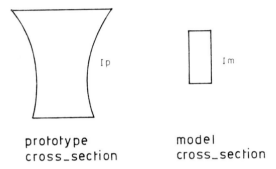

prototype   model
cross_section   cross_section

Fig. 3.4.   Distorted models are often necessary. An intricate cross-section of a beam may be simulated by simple cross-section giving rise to a distorted model based on flexural similarity.

It is usual to apply a uniform distortion over the entire model, as in a shell model with a different thickness-scale ratio to length-scale ratio. However, dissimilar distortions of sections of the model have been made; even though the actual model thickness may remain constant the prototype thickness varies. An actual model with varying distortion is described in Section 8.3.

This process effectively expands the usefulness of model results if the stresses in some segment of the model are found to give stresses too high for the prototype. The prototype is thickened or made stiffer by altering the corresponding scale ratios, and the same set of model results is used to calculate new stresses in the prototype.

3.20. *Model Types and Similarity*

Many aspects of architecture remain descriptive in spite of the application of operations research techniques to architectural planning and decision-making. However, architectural philosophy is being rationalised [3.16 and 3.17], and it is to be expected that effort in the social, behavioural and environmental spheres will increase architectural definition.

In the architectural system eight groups of variable can be separated [3.18]:

Visual design
Town planning
Functional planning
Constructional
Structural
Thermal
Acoustical
Lighting.

Since it is not practical to study all the eight sub-systems simultaneously, we consider a limited number of variables at any one time; *e.g.* a sub-group within a sub-system. Model types are classified by the predominant variables.

Visual design models (Section 6.2) are used to quantify design concepts and as an aid to explaining the design to others. Geometrical similarity is the prime requirement.

Town planning models (Section 6.3) are used to study relationships between the various components in a three dimensional panorama. Geometrical similarity is the prime requirement.

Functional planning models (Section 6.4) usually take the form of partial or transparent models in which detailed planning of services integration, furniture placement and other requirements are studied. Geometrical similarity is required.

Constructional models (Section 6.5) are used to study fabrication techniques; *e.g.* jointing details of repetitive components. Trial erection of a full scale section of the building is often worthwhile. Geometrical similarity is essential and often physical similarity is needed.

Structural models (Section 8.5) are employed to study complex structures and the effects of complex external actions such as wind and earthquake. Complete similarity is desirable, but distorted models are often useful. Analogues can also be used.

Thermal models (Sections 7.9 and 7.10) are used to study the thermal performance of buildings as well as the subjective and physiological effects of thermal environment. Complete similarity is required. Analogues are often used.

Acoustical models (Sections 7.14 and 7.15) for studying the acoustical performance of buildings. Geometrical similarity and a degree of physical similarity is required. Analogues are often used.

Lighting models (Section 7.17) are used to investigate natural and artificial lighting conditions. Geometrical similarity is of prime importance; often some physical similarity is also required.

PROBLEMS

3.1 An undistorted model of an interconnected beam system has been designed with the following prototype : model ratios

$$\lambda_l \ 5 : 1$$
$$\lambda_E \ 2 : 1$$
$$\lambda_\mu \ 1 : 1.$$

Find the prototype : model ratios for loads, stresses and deflections.

3.2 If the maximum principal stress at a point in the model of a grid system is 5,000 lb/sq in, calculate the magnitude of the maximum principal stress at the corresponding point in the prototype of material with a modulus of elasticity of 30×10^6 lb/sq in and Poisson's ratio of 0·3. The prototype : model ratio for linear dimensions is 5, and for loads it is 50. The model material has a modulus of elasticity of 600,000 lb/sq in and a Poisson's ratio of 0·36. (*University of New South Wales, 1961.*)

3.3 A model of a four-bay, three-storey structure is constructed to determine the elastic deflections of the prototype under load. Prototype : model ratios are

$$\lambda_l \quad 12 : 1$$
$$\lambda_I \quad 1000 : 1$$
$$\lambda_W \quad 100 : 1$$
$$\lambda_E \quad 3 : 1.$$

What would be the ratio of deflections in the prototype to that in the model for corresponding loads?

3.4 A small tower-like structure is to be tested using a model. It has the following prototype quantities:

height of columns	40 ft
radius at top	160 ft
differential foundation settlement	2 in
modulus of elasticity (concrete)	3×10^6 lb/sq in
live load	130 lb/sq ft

It is decided to choose scale ratios of 1 : 20 for the column lengths and 1 : 8 for the modulus of elasticity. How are the other properties to be scaled?

Answers

3.1   50 : 1; 2 : 1; 5 : 1
3.2   380 lb/sq in
3.3   57·5 : 1
3.4   height of columns 1 : 20, model columns = 2 ft
       radius at top 1 : 20, model radius = 8 ft
       differential foundation settlement 1 : 120
       model differential settlement = 0·1 in
       live load 1 : 8, model live load = 16·25 lb/sq ft.

Chapter 4

Construction of Structural Models

4.1. Early Models

An outline of the historical development of the structural model has been given in Chapter 2. In one of the earliest treatises on architecture [4.1] the Renaissance architect Leone Alberti (1404–1472) wrote:

"No Man ought to begin a Building hastily, but should first take a good deal of Time to consider, and resolve in his Mind all the Qualities and Requisites of such a Work. And that he should carefully review and examine, with the Advice of proper Judges, the whole Structure in itself, and the Proportions and Measures of every distinct Part, not only in Draughts or Paintings, but in actual Models of Wood or some other Substance, that when he has finish'd his Building, he may not repent of his Labour. . . .

"You ought to make such Models, and consider them by yourself, and with others so diligently, and examine them over and over so often, that there shall not be a single Part in your whole Structure, but what you are thoroughly acquainted with."

To be sure, the precision of early models is open to question, but then the achievements must be considered relative to the science and technology of the age. The important point is that there should be this spirit of enquiry into problems unknown or uncertain. Insofar as Galileo and Newton sought, by observation, to improve the basic Truths of science they were in effect opening the first chapter on experimental structures. Through sophistication in the techniques of experimentation the *structural* model has today become the most advanced model type employed in building design and construction.

At the present stage of its development, the structural model is widely accepted by design engineers and architects, and more importantly, by many public authorities having jurisdiction over the design of structures. Dimensional analysis has now reached an advanced level of development and will continue to serve the analysis and planning of structural model studies; but further research is necessary on the practical aspects of developing suitable model materials, on methods of manufacture as well as on the techniques of loading and measurement.

4.2. Types of Structural Model

Structural model studies may be conveniently divided into three main types, depending upon the principal objectives of the investigation.

Behavioural models are designed to demonstrate clearly some particular structural behaviour or principle. In order to do this well, it is often found advantageous to exaggerate the response of the model to various actions, by deliberately simulating extreme conditions or using model materials which magnify the structural response. Behavioural models are used as a teaching aid to complement analytical instruction [4 ?] and as a medium for the preliminary semi-quantitative assessment of complex structures. Emphasis on the visualisation of the desired behaviour is often accompanied by a suppression of unwanted secondary effects; *i.e.* deliberately distorting similarity relationships. Therefore behavioural or demonstration models are generally simple physical contrivances demanding much ingenuity of design, but a minimum of labour and expense. When the study forms part of the evaluation of early structural concepts for a design, behavioural models are invaluable, *e.g.* during the early phase of the design of a stadium, as they help to resolve the potentiality and feasibility of alternative structural concepts.

Fig. 4.1 shows a 1 : 48 scale model made by the structural engineers; the material is balsa wood, and no special skill or facilities were required for construction.

For teaching purposes, behavioural models may be made of almost any material. For instance, moderately stiff paper is suitable for a convincing demonstration of the strength gain of slab structures by folding, and a block of foamed plastic can transform the rather abstract idea of the "middle third law" into a more lasting physical image for the novice in structural mechanics. Hence wood, metal and plastics have all found application. Cotton threads can be used to simulate cross bracing in cardboard models.

The impact of behavioural models has influenced the philosophy of teaching structural principles to students of architecture and related disciplines. Teachers of architectural science have found this approach rewarding and this aspect of model studies has, since its introduction [4.3] become an important part of the architectural science laboratory. Benefits accruing from such model studies should not, however, be exaggerated to the detriment of a proper analytical understanding.

Fig. 4.1.   Balsa wood behavioural model of plated dome structure manufactured by the consulting engineer to determine overall pattern of deflections. (*See* Fig. 8.5 for plastic structural model.)

Confirmatory models, as the name implies, provide correlative evidence for analytical methods and are usually conducted when circumstances are such that:

(i) the theoretical analysis is available, but the degree of uncertainty of the approximations made in the formulation and solution of the theory is not known; and

(ii) an acceptable design method is available, but the magnitude and importance of the structure warrant an experimental verification.

Case (i) includes model studies on the acceptability of existing methods of theoretical analysis and the testing of improved mathematical formulations. It is therefore essential that the physical model is similar to the mathematical model, rather than to reality. This simplifies the problem as attention is focussed on the confirmation of an analytical solution, which, if successful, is modified and extended to cover the real physical system more accurately. For example, in a study of the elastic theory of thin concrete shell structures it is preferable to select a near-elastic and homogeneous material like Plexiglas for the model in spite of its dissimilarity to reinforced concrete.

Case (ii) arises when the prototype structure is very expensive or the consequences of failure are disastrous, *e.g.* a tower structure of unprecedented proportion or a containment vessel in a nuclear energy generating establishment. A successful model correlation then provides a "second opinion" to theory, and raises the level of confidence in the subsequent structural design. For instance, the structural design of the 1,250 ft (380 m) high Empire State Building, built in 1933, was aided by a wind tunnel model study to check the magnitude and nature of the wind forces [4.4]. Fig. 4.2 shows the proof testing of a full-scale model of a component of the shell roof system employed in the Sydney Opera House.

Design models are the most expensive type. Architectural structures are intrinsically complex, and the separation of a structure into beams, columns and cladding is but an approximation born of expediency. While this simplification serves to render analytical design methods practicable, it is acceptable only as long as the results are consistent. If the approximation is excessive, either a grossly conservative or a dangerously unsafe structure results. If the structure is too difficult for an analytical solution, it is best to use a design model.

Direct structural design on the basis of models is widely used for the design of aero-structures and dams. Aero-structures demand safety as well as minimum weight, while dams must be made safe in spite of the complex interaction between structure and supporting strata. Applications to building structures have not been so spectacular, although they are gaining in significance as buildings become more daring. Direct design models are useful for highly indeterminate structures such as grid and tower structures. Their outstanding application is to complex shell shapes, which are not expressible mathematically or have difficult boundary conditions, *e.g.* the model analysis of the Eastman Kodak Pavilion [4.5] for the 1964 New York World's Fair (Fig. 4.3).

Fig. 4.2. Full scale testing of components of roof system employed in the Sydney Opera House (*Ove Arup and Partners*).

Fig. 4.3. Architectural model of the Eastman Kodak Pavilion, 1964 New York World Fair, indicating complexity of roof (*Dr. L. Zetlin*).

Before making a model study the basis for design, three factors must be considered:

(i)   availability of specialised facilities and personnel to ensure good reliability of test results obtained;

(ii) acceptability of this method of design to the building authorities; and

(iii) competitiveness in terms of time and money by comparison with an analytical method (if feasible).

Currently, model analyses are conducted mainly by specialised university, governmental and commercial laboratories which have built up, over a number of years, the requisite facilities and expertise. The time and money required for an adequate model investigation depends on the accuracy required; but in complex problems particularly, the model study may suggest improvements in the design far in excess of the cost.

4.3. Structural Forms and Actions

Structural forms (Fig. 4.4) are classified according to the dimensionality of the structure at large:

(i)   one-dimensional, *e.g.* a single cable;

(ii) two-dimensional, *e.g.* a slab; and

(iii) three-dimensional, *e.g.* a curved surface structure.

A structure must be taken as a structural entity, and an integrated spatial assemblage of one-dimensional elements, *e.g.* a space grid, is properly a three-dimensional structure.

Structural actions, by contrast, describe the internal behaviour of the structure. Therefore a cable is a one-dimensional stress system, whereas slabs and thin shells are two-dimensional stress systems. "Thick" shells, however, have a three-dimensional state of stress.

States of stress. The theory of elasticity is covered by numerous texts [4.6] and it is proposed to state only the equations essential to structural model investigations, without proof.

STRUCTURE	DIMENSIONAL ORDER	
	FORM	ACTION
CABLE 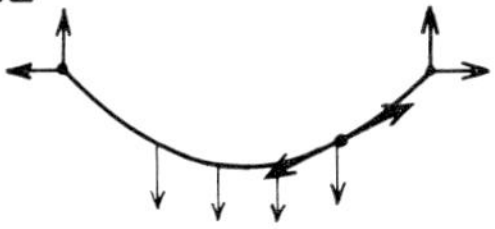	1 - D	1 - D
BEAM 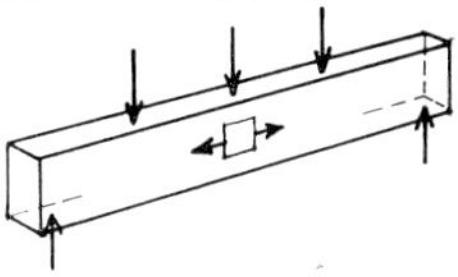	1 - D	1 - D
SLAB 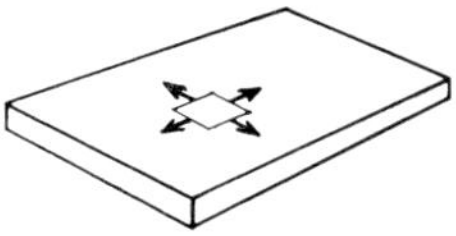	2 - D	2 - D
THIN SHELL 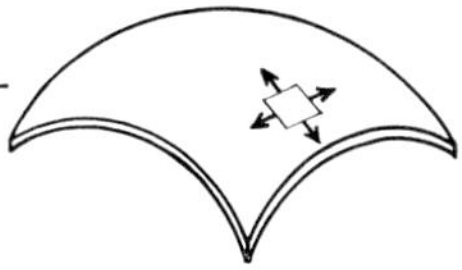	3 - D	2 - D
2-LAYER GRID 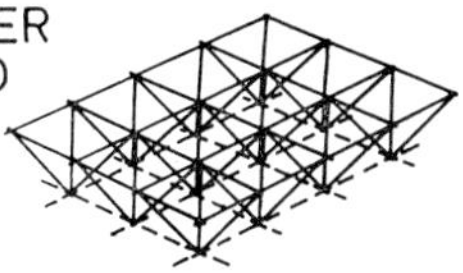	3 - D	1 - D
SPACE GRID 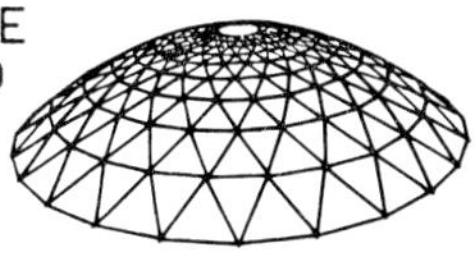	3 - D	1 - D

Fig. 4.4. Structural forms and actions. Structural forms are classified according to the dimensionality of the structure; structural actions describe the internal action of the structure.

Imagine that we have a small cubical element of a structure consisting of an elastic, homogeneous and isotropic material (Fig. 4.5). Let the co-ordinate axes of reference x, y, z, be chosen so that the shear stresses vanish (principal directions) and consider the following states of stress.

(i) *One-dimensional stress state* obtains if only the normal stress σ_x is present (Fig. 4.5 (a)).

(ii) *Two-dimensional stress state* obtains if two normal stresses σ_x and σ_y act simultaneously on the cube. This is also described as a "plane stress" condition (Fig. 4.5(b)).

(iii) *Three-dimensional stress state* obtains with three normal stresses, σ_x, σ_y and σ_z (Fig. 4.5(c)).

The normal stresses acting in the principal directions include the maximum positive and negative stresses, and are therefore those of practical significance to design.

Consider the action of σ_x alone. By Hooke's law the component strains are

$$\varepsilon_{x1} = \frac{1}{E} \cdot \sigma_x; \qquad \varepsilon_{y1} = -\frac{\mu}{E} \sigma_x = \varepsilon_{z1} \qquad (4.1a)$$

Similarly, for σ_x and σ_z acting separately,

$$\varepsilon_{y2} = \frac{1}{E} \sigma_y; \qquad \varepsilon_{z2} = -\frac{\mu}{E} \sigma_y = \varepsilon_{x2} \qquad (4.1b)$$

$$\varepsilon_{z3} = \frac{1}{E} \sigma_z; \qquad \varepsilon_{x3} = -\frac{\mu}{E} \sigma_z = \varepsilon_{y3} \qquad (4.1c)$$

The effects of σ_x, σ_y and σ_z may be superimposed because the equations are linear, giving total normal strains equal to

$$\varepsilon_x = \varepsilon_{x1} + \varepsilon_{x2} + \varepsilon_{x3}$$

$$= \frac{1}{E} \sigma_x - \frac{\mu}{E} \sigma_y - \frac{\mu}{E} \sigma_z$$

$$= \frac{1}{E} \{\sigma_x - \mu(\sigma_y + \sigma_z)\} \qquad (4.2a)$$

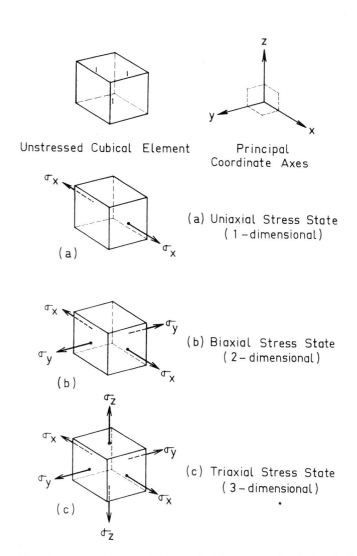

Unstressed Cubical Element

Principal
Coordinate Axes

(a) Uniaxial Stress State
(1 –dimensional)

(b) Biaxial Stress State
(2 – dimensional)

(c) Triaxial Stress State
(3 – dimensional)

Fig. 4.5.   The three basic states of stress: uniaxial stress state in which only the normal stress, σ_x, acts; biaxial stress state in which two normal stresses, σ_x and σ_y, act; and triaxial stress state in which three normal stresses, σ_x, σ_y and σ_z, act.

and similarly,

$$\varepsilon_y = \frac{1}{E}\left\{\sigma_y - \mu(\sigma_x+\sigma_z)\right\} \qquad (4.2b)$$

$$\varepsilon_z = \frac{1}{E}\left\{\sigma_z - \mu(\sigma_x+\sigma_y)\right\}. \qquad (4.2c)$$

Equations (4.1) and (4.2) are greatly simplified if Poisson's ratio vanishes. However, practical materials of construction usually have values of the order of 0·15 to 0·35 and this must be recognised when interpreting model strains.

4.4. Model Materials

The whole range of materials used in structural models is as large as that used for the prototypes. Four major types will be briefly discussed, viz. paper and wood, plastics, cementitious materials and metals. In making a decision, the following should be considered:

(i)   strength characteristics
(ii)   failure characteristics
(iii)   creep characteristics
(iv)   temperature and humidity effects
(v)   influences of loading procedures
(vi)   size effect
(vii)   workability.

It is always necessary to determine the quantitative properties essential to the problem, particularly for materials, such as plastics and concretes, which show high variability from sample to sample.

The strength characteristics are important, and for elastic model studies, the modulus of elasticity, Poisson's ratio and the limit of proportionality are required. Ultimate behaviour can only be studied if the stress–strain curve is known to the point of failure. Creep characteristics are necessary to estimate time-dependent deflections, which influence the rate of loading and the sequence of measurements. Temperature and humidity affect the strength and creep properties of many materials, and model studies under constant temperature and humidity are to be preferred. If inelastic behaviour is to be studied, the superposition principle no longer holds true, and it becomes necessary to consider the sequence of applying the various loads to the model.

The failure of a brittle or fibrous material is dependent on the size of the test specimen, and this *size-effect* is pertinent to model studies [4.7]. Wood and concrete show considerable size-effects.

Finally, machinability of the model material must be given the most careful consideration, since it determines the cost and effort required to achieve an acceptable standard of accuracy, and even the feasibility of the project.

Paper and paperboards are extensively used for qualitative models for demonstration and feasibility studies because of their ready availability and ease of working. The strength properties of paper products are directional and highly variable and the materials are greatly affected by humidity, which precludes their use in structural investigations.

Wood and wood products are versatile materials because of their availability, good machinability and ease of assembly. However, the strength characteristics of wood are highly directional with respect to grain direction which renders it unsuitable as an accurate model material for prototypes other than timber structures. When used in structural models, the pronounced effects of moisture content, temperature, shrinkage, and creep must be taken into account.

Decreasing moisture content tends to increase the strength properties of wood. A one per cent change in moisture content causes the following percentage changes in properties [4.8]:

static bending: fibre stress at rupture	4 per cent
modulus of elasticity	2 per cent
crushing strength parallel to grain	6 per cent
shear strength parallel to grain	3 per cent.

A temperature increase of 1°C causes approximately a 1·0 per cent decrease of all strength properties.

Balsa wood, like paperboard, is suitable for demonstration and feasibility model studies, but its directional variability is even greater than that of normal wood. *Plywood* and hardboard have more uniform properties and are less affected by moisture content and shrink-

Table 4.1
Properties of plastics

Property	Acrylic resins (Perspex, Lucite, Plexiglas)	Cellulose nitrate (Celluloid)	Phenolics (Bakelite)	Polyester resin	Epoxy resin	Polyvinyl-chloride
Classification	thermoplastic	thermoplastic	thermosetting	thermosetting	thermosetting	thermoplastic
Modulus of elasticity lb/sq in	$4 \cdot 5 \times 10^5$	$0 \cdot 65\text{--}40 \times 10^5$	$5 \cdot 5\text{--}7 \cdot 5 \times 10^5$	$3 \cdot 0\text{--}5 \cdot 5 \times 10^5$	$2 \cdot 0\text{--}6 \cdot 0 \times 10^5$	$4 \cdot 0\text{--}5 \cdot 0 \times 10^5$
Poisson's ratio	$0 \cdot 36$	$0 \cdot 41$	$0 \cdot 36$	$0 \cdot 40$	$0 \cdot 40$	$0 \cdot 40$
Tensile strength lb/sq in	8,000–10,000	3,000–7,000	7,000–15,000	3,500–10,000	5,000–12,000	5,000–10,000
Compressive strength lb/sq in	12,000–20,000	3,000–30,000	10,000–25,000	12,000–20,000	15,000–30,000	10,000–12,000
Elongation at rupture, per cent	3–10	40–90	1	5	5–10	2–40
Softening point °C	80–98	70	—	—	—	82
Coeff. of linear expansion cm °C/cm	$5\text{--}9 \times 10^{-5}$	$11\text{--}17 \times 10^{-5}$	4×10^{-5}	6×10^{-5}	$5\text{--}9 \times 10^{-5}$	5×10^{-5}
Machinability	Excellent	Excellent	Good	Fair	Good	Excellent

age and are often useful as a material for large experimental structures.

The average shrinkage from a soaked to an oven-dry condition of 3-ply panels having all plies of the same thickness and same species of wood is 0·45 per cent parallel to the face grain, and 0·67 per cent perpendicular to the face grain.

The properties of the plywood panel as a whole can be computed from the properties of the individual layers [ref. 4.8, pp. 281–285].

Solid plastics are amongst the most common materials used for structural models. Their more important properties are given in Table 4.1 [4.9 and 4.10].

In addition to the properties outlined, translucent plastics possess unique optical qualities which make them suitable for photoelastic model investigation (*see* Section 2.7).

Acrylic resins, cellulose nitrate and polyvinyl chloride are *thermoplastics*, that is they soften when heated and can be remoulded. Phenolics, polyester resins and epoxy resins are *thermosets* which once set do not soften to allow remoulding.

Most of the plastics used for model making are reasonably homogeneous and isotropic; but their stress–strain relation does not conform to Hooke's law, the strain being a function of the time of the loading cycle as well as stress. This *creep* factor must be allowed for in the experimental technique. Most of the plastics employed for models are almost perfectly visco-elastic, *i.e.* the stress–strain relation at any instant after loading is linear although the modulus of elasticity varies with time. This behaviour is illustrated in Fig. 4.6 [4.11].

The difficulties arising from these time-dependent effects may be overcome either by deferring the measurements until the increase of strain with time is very small (but this is a time-consuming procedure), or by taking measurements at a specified time interval after loading. It is important to ensure that there is no appreciable creep during the time necessary to take the measurements. Determination of material properties must, of course, be carried out at the same length of time after loading as the measurements. Rocha [4.11] has described a method for obtaining a considerable number of readings from a model of visco-elastic materials by cycling the load until the observed strain difference between loading and unloading becomes constant (Fig. 4.7). The material now behaves as if it were elastic, with an effective elastic modulus based on the strain difference between the commencement of loading and the beginning of the following unloading.

The time dependence of the strain creates difficulty in establishing a datum for the measurements, since the strain at any given time

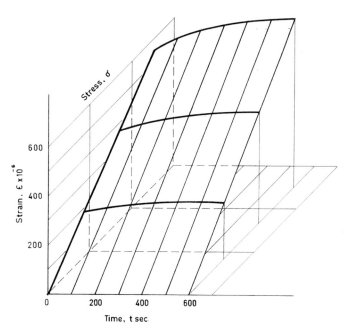

Fig. 4.6.   Creep surface for alkathene indicating its visco-elastic behaviour (*after Rocha* [4.11]).

depends on the stress history as well as the applied stress in the material at that time. This is often called the *elastic memory* of the plastic. It is desirable to leave sufficient time between loading cycles to allow the creep strain to recover. For practical purposes, this is achieved if the model is left unloaded longer than the duration of the previous loading application.

The elastic constants and strength of plastics are susceptible to *temperature variations*, and this is of value in forming operations. For

Perspex (Plexiglas, Lucite) an increase in temperature results in a decrease of the elastic modulus and strength (at 20°C, approximately 1 per cent per °C). Poisson's ratio for Perspex remains essentially constant with variations in temperature. It is desirable that all testing be carried out in temperature controlled environments; the effect of humidity on plastics is sufficiently small to be negligible.

The most commonly used plastic for models is methyl methacrylate, one of the acrylic resins; it is manufactured commercially as *Perspex, Plexiglas or Lucite* in sheets of various thickness. It is important to check the thickness of the sheets at a number of points;

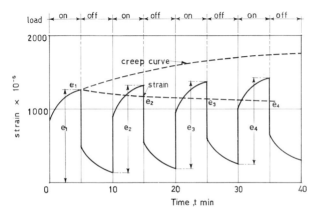

Fig. 4.7. Repeated loading of a visco-elastic material showing constant strain increment after first loading cycle (*after Rocha* [4.11]).

if the variation in thickness is greater than a few thousandths of an inch, corresponding corrections must be made to the cross-sectional dimensions of the model (*see* Section 8.3).

Rigid plastic foams are well suited for demonstration models and qualitative studies. Whilst they have the desirable properties of low moduli of elasticity (as low as 600 lb/sq in or 42 kg/sq cm) and are readily machined, large local variations of the elastic properties [4.12] make quantitative stress distribution studies difficult.

Micro-concrete is made by a geometrical scaling down of the grading curve of the prototype constituents of concrete. This is feasible with the larger aggregates, which scale to a sand-cement mortar. Fig. 4.8 shows the grading curve of two micro-concretes reported by Johnson [4.13] and Figs. 4.9 and 4.10 indicate good agreement between the strength of two scaled-down mixes over an appreciable range. If the model test cylinder is determined from the prototype cylinder by scaling in the same ratio as the structure, the test samples are frequently too small to test (*e.g.* $\frac{1}{8}$ in × $\frac{1}{4}$ in or 3 mm × 6 mm). However, before altering the cylinder size, account must be taken of the *size effect*: as the cylinder size becomes smaller, so the result obtained for strength increases [4.14 and 4.15]. It is advisable to determine the mortar strength using three different test cylinder

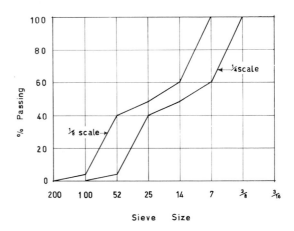

Fig. 4.8. Grading curve for aggregates in eighth- and quarter-scale micro-concrete mixes shown as percentage passing British Standard sieves (*after Johnson* [4.13]).

sizes, and to extrapolate or interpolate to obtain the correct model material strength. For micro-concretes employing sand:cement ratios in the range 2·5:1 to 4:1 and water:cement ratios in the range of 0·4:1 to 0·55:1, strengths from about 4,000 to 10,000 lb/sq in (280–700 kg/sq cm) can be obtained in 28 days. The elastic modulus and Poisson's ratio of the material are about the same as those of a normal concrete having the same strength.

Epoxy–sand mixtures are formed by replacing the cement in micro-concrete with epoxy resin. The sand reduces the time-dependent properties (*i.e.* creep of the plastic) and often permits a useful variation of specific weight, Poisson's ratio and modulus of elasticity. However, it cannot be used for ultimate strength studies because of its relatively high tensile strength.

Pumice–cement mortars developed by the ISMES laboratories [4.16] consist of graded pumice and cement, with powdered limestone and other additives in smaller quantities. Their usefulness lies

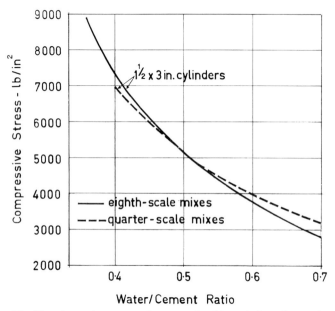

Fig. 4.9. The change in compressive strength with variation of water/cement ratio for eighth- and quarter-scale micro-concrete mixes.

in the ability to vary the modulus of elasticity and Poisson's ratio. The value of the modulus of elasticity can range from 2,000 to 150,000 lb/sq in (140–10,500 kg/sq cm) together with a Poisson's ratio of 0·18 to 0·20. The model is coated with a sealant to prevent egress of water, since shrinkage effects are large. The similarity of the stress–strain relation and creep characteristics of pumice–cement mortars to those of concrete makes them suitable for model testing to failure.

Adding a heavy granular material such as litharge, iron or magnesite, produces a heavy mortar with a modular ratio (λ_E) and a specific mass ratio (λ_ρ) of the order of 150 and 1·5, respectively. Therefore, from the similitude condition

$$\lambda_\rho = \frac{\lambda_E}{\lambda_l}.$$

λ_l is capable of taking a value up to about 100. This is desirable for ultimate strength models of structures where proper distribution

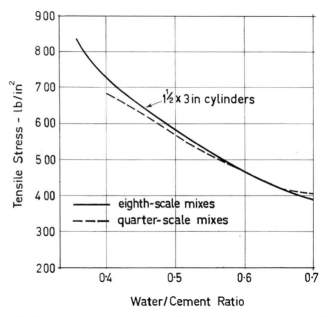

Fig. 4.10. The change in tensile strength with variation of water/cement ratio for eighth- and quarter-scale micro-concrete mixes.

of self-weight is of paramount importance (*e.g.* a dam or a shell structure under earthquake loading). It is possible to change the value of the stress scale factor for any part of the model either by increasing the litharge content or by injecting cement grout.

Asbestos cement sheet is valuable in the study of elastic plate problems: it has a modulus of elasticity and Poisson's ratio essentially the same as concrete, *i.e.* 4,800,000 lb/sq in (340,000 kg/sq cm) and 0·15, respectively. It is available in sheet form with very small tolerances.

Plaster of Paris (*gypsum*) is a suitable substitute for the cement mortar of micro-concretes; it is also used extensively plain or with the addition of admixtures, and has the advantage of an early initial setting time (about 10 minutes), thus speeding up the manufacture of the model. It also renders subsequent tests on modified models a practicable proposition; the modifications may be made by a simple process of filling or grinding off. The elastic properties of Plaster of Paris are strongly dependent on age, temperature and humidity [4.17, 4.18 and 4.19]. Lee and Coates [4.20] found negligible variation of elastic properties with time after about 20 days. Fig. 4.11 shows the variation of the elastic modulus with water: plastic ratio; little variation is apparent in the value of Poisson's ratio with changes in water: plaster ratio, and it has a value of approximately 0·16 to 0·20 depending on age. This is very close to that of concrete (0·15 to 0·20).

The stress–strain curve of plaster with additives (usually diatomaceous earth) is similar to that of concrete, and it may be used for both elastic and inelastic tests since the additives tend to lower the tensile strength to about one-sixth of the compressive strength; this is considerably lower than that for plain plaster (about one-quarter) [4.21].

Reinforcement for models presents a number of problems; the extreme smallness of size usually means that wires must be used, and these must be straightened. This process of straightening generally destroys the yield point of the material; straightened wires exhibit a definite yield point again after ageing or hot-working.

Sometimes it is impossible to find a small-diameter wire with a yield strength equal to that of mild steel reinforcement. It is then best to replace several prototype bars by a single wire in the model. The load carried by the model wire at failure must obey the laws of similitude so that

$$\pi \, r_m{}^2 \, \sigma_m = \lambda_E \, \lambda_l{}^2 \, k \, \pi \, r_p{}^2 \, \sigma_p \qquad (4.3)$$

where r_m is the radius of model reinforcement, r_p is the radius of prototype reinforcement, σ_m is the model yield stress used to represent k prototype bars, and σ_p is the prototype yield stress of bars.

If the steel to concrete bond strength is u, then similitude of bond forces requires that

$$2\,\pi.r_m\,u_m = \lambda_E\,\lambda_l\,k.2\,\pi.r_p\,u_p. \tag{4.4}$$

It follows from equations (4.3) and (4.4) that

$$\frac{\sigma_m}{\sigma_p} = \lambda_l\,\frac{r_p}{r_m}.\frac{u_m}{u_p} \tag{4.5}$$

For given values of λ_E, λ_l, σ_m, σ_p, u_m, u_p and r_p, the value of r_m can be computed from eqn. (4.5). The value of k then follows from either eqn. (4.3) or (4.4). Prototype bond strengths have been

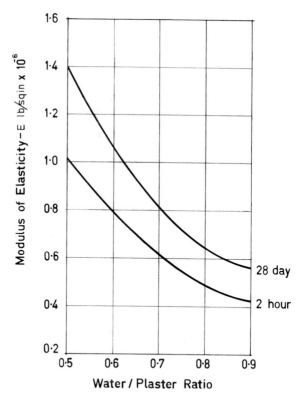

Fig. 4.11. The effect of water/plaster ratio on the elastic modulus of gypsum (*after Russell and Blakey* [4.18]).

determined by Mathey and Watstein [4.22] and by Menzel and Woods [4.23].

Steel is not used extensively as reinforcement in model tests because of the high loads required by its high modulus of elasticity; machining and jointing require specialized skills (*e.g.* welding), although annealed threaded mild steel rods have been used [4.19].

Phosphor bronze wire, when annealed, gives a definite yield point; this, combined with its lower modulus of elasticity and good machinability makes it suitable for modelling intermediate grade steel reinforcement [4.24].

4.5. Construction of Models

Model construction, like building construction, requires careful pre-planning and skilled execution which can only be attained by experience. The limitations on the usage of otherwise suitable model materials of construction is of major importance, and these inhibiting factors are combinations of availability of proper tools and skilled personnel, and the exigencies of time and cost.

Model construction techniques may be classified under:

(i)   cut-out
(ii) assembly
(iii) thermal forming
(iv) casting
(v)   spin forming.

4.5.1. CUT-OUT TECHNIQUES.—These are most suited to planar models; acrylic plastics (Perspex, Plexiglas, Lucite) are the most often used model material in this case because of their low elastic modulus, relatively low cost and good machinability. They are commercially available in sheets, rods and tubes and may be machined using wood- or metal-working equipment. Cutting is the most common operation, but drilling and trimming are also sometimes needed during model manufacture.

Cutting with high speed band saws or circular saws is in general the best method of cutting acrylic plastics. Large band saws have the advantage that, owing to the length of the blade, frictional heat is dissipated before any part of the saw comes into contact with the work a second time and thus faster cutting is possible. In addition, with band saws cutting is not restricted to straight lines. Circular saws, on the other hand, are preferable for the cutting of strips and straight edges. *Band saw* blades as used for light metals, having 10 to 20 teeth per inch (4 to 8 teeth per cm) and a running speed of 5,000 ft (1,500 m) or more per minute are suitable. The saw guides should be kept as close together as possible in order to reduce the tendency for the blade to twist; this ensures straight cutting and longer life for the blade. *Circular saws* should be hollow ground; for most work, saw blades made from high-speed steel and machine-sharpened are adequate. The pitch of the saw should vary with the thickness of the sheet to be cut, varying from 8 to 10 teeth per inch (3–4 teeth per cm) for $\frac{1}{8}$-inch (3-mm) Perspex, up to 3 to 5 teeth per inch (1–2 teeth per cm) for $\frac{1}{2}$-inch (12.7 mm) Perspex or over. The blade peripheral speed should be of the order of 10,000 ft per minute (3,000 m per minute) or over. Adequate power must be available to ensure that there is no reduction of speed during cutting. For example, with a 10-inch (25-cm) diameter blade, a motor of at least 3 h.p. should be used. *Jig saws* can be used to cut small pieces of Perspex, but they are not generally used because the process is slow and the saw tends to become over-heated very easily causing the plastic to melt.

Drilling of plastics can be carried out on standard equipment using ordinary twist drills, but those with slow spiral and wide flutes will make good work easier to achieve. It is important to avoid overheating, and it is therefore advisable to use a hand feed so that the swarf can be cleared frequently, and binding and gumming do not occur. The speed of the drill is not critical and the following figures can be used as a guide:

$\frac{1}{16}$-inch (1·6-mm) diameter 6,000 r.p.m.

$\frac{1}{4}$-inch (6·4-mm) diameter 1,800 r.p.m.

$\frac{1}{2}$-inch (12·7-mm) diameter   900 r.p.m.

Drills should have no rake and a clearance angle of about 15°–20°. The use of an efficient cooling system is vital to the production of accurate strain-free holes. Any proprietary soluble cutting oil may be safely used, but a strong air jet is efficacious and avoids the need for subsequent cleaning.

Milling of plastics can be carried out in the same manner as that for light metals, but for the best results particular care must be taken to adequately hold the work in position. Tools with wide pitch, no front rake, and adequate back clearance are desirable [4.25].

4.5.2. ASSEMBLY TECHNIQUES.—These rely on their jointing for their effectiveness. For acrylic plastics *capillary cementing* (or welding) is the most widely used method of joining two members. Adjoining pieces are held firmly and the plastic solvent (usually acetone, but any ketone or ester may be used, also some alcohols) is applied to the joint using a hypodermic needle; capillary action draws the solvent into the joint, the plastic is dissolved, and finally the solvent evaporates to produce a uniform joint. This type of cementing is particularly useful as it requires no application of heat to aid polymerization; furthermore inspection of the joint in transparent plastics is very simple. *Epoxy resin cements* are also used in model manufacture because of their relative ease of application and their extremely high strength. It is supplied as two components: a plasticizer and an accelerator (or hardener); the hardening time may be varied by varying the proportions or by increasing the temperature.

Furthermore, these adjustments in proportions allow a variation in the modulus of elasticity of the cement from 3×10^4 to 3×10^6 lb/sq inch. Epoxy resin cements can also be used to join segments of timber and metal models. Thin sheets of polyvinyl chloride and laminated thermoplastic sheets can be joined by welding of the two surfaces by applying heat locally (use is made of the welding iron). This process is applicable to models of pneumatic structures (and to the manufacture of the air bags used for loading, as described in Section 5.8).

Brazing and silver soldering take the place of welding in metal models as electric arc welding, at reduced scales, is very difficult. Tests on silver-soldered joints, in a model using annealed phosphor bronze, compared very well with the prototype steel results where the connections were arc-welded.

Mechanical jointing is generally only used when the available area is insufficient for cementing to be effective, and yet high stresses have to be maintained. This occurs in models of prestressed concrete structures in the prestressing system, and in models of cable structures (Fig. 4.12). Most mechanical joints rely on frictional forces to be effective; however, care must be taken as stress concentrations are not produced in the member at this point.

4.5.3. THERMAL FORMING TECHNIQUES.—These are used extensively with thermo-plastics, particularly polyvinyl chloride (PVC), cellulose acetate, and polymethyl methacrylate to produce three-dimensional models. The existence of the "rubbery stage", before complete melting, in the heating of thermoplastics is the characteristic which makes them suitable for forming models in this manner.

Fig. 4.12.   Mechanical jointing of 0·024 inch diameter wires in the model of a cable suspension structure.

Drape forming of shells with single curvature is the simplest of thermal forming techniques, polymethyl methacrylate generally being used. The plastic sheet and the mould are heated in a controlled oven to 125°C; this is the temperature at which the plastic becomes completely rubbery, loses its ability to support itself and drapes onto the mould. The oven temperature is slowly lowered since uneven cooling of the two sides of the sheet produces significant "bowing" of the final product. Very shallow shells of double curvature may also be produced by this process (Fig. 4.13). If sudden changes in curvature are required, such as in a hipped barrel shell, an additional mating mould is employed and pressure used to force the plastic into the Vee; polymethyl methacrylate is not well suited for this latter process and PVC may be used.

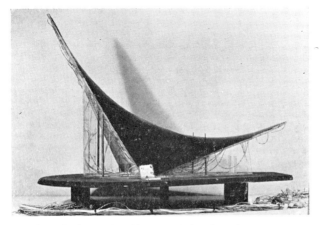

Fig. 4.13.   A hyperbolic–paraboloid polymethylmethacrylate shell formed by the drape technique.

Vacuum forming is needed to produce models with double curvature, since plastic will not stretch in two directions under its own weight alone. Various techniques are utilised, including blowing the rubbery sheet into a female mould and vacuuming into a female mould (Fig. 4.14); a similar procedure can be applied to a male mould. If necessary a companion mould can be used to produce local changes in geometry. Varying rates of cooling of different areas of the model resulting from uneven heating can lead to large residual stresses. Vacuum forming tends to stretch and thin the material in certain regions of the model more than others. The degree of this change in cross-sectional area is largely governed by the shape of the structure being modelled and the sudden changes of geometry involved; these changes in thickness in large models are hard to measure [4.26].

Moulds for drape forming are usually made of timber (Fig. 4.15), either machined in one piece or made up in segments and joined together. Particular care must be taken with timber moulds if they are to be re-used, because of the dimensional changes associated with changes in moisture content of the timber. Plaster of Paris is often used as a moulding material because of the ease of working it. Moulds for vacuum forming are often made of metal although this is very expensive.

Fig. 4.14. A triangulated spherical polymethylmethacrylate shell formed using the vacuum technique.

Equipment required for drape forming includes a temperature-controlled oven large enough to handle the model; equipment for vacuum-forming include 100 lb/sq inch air pressure systems to produce the required vacuum, and thermal coils with the associated electrical control equipment. Whilst size is not a limitation to vacuum-forming equipment, the cost increases approximately as the square of the model dimensions. For this reason recourse is generally made to commercial manufacture of the model, since vacuum forming is well established for commercial applications.

4.5.4. CASTING TECHNIQUES.—These are used with *epoxy resin plastics* such as Araldite and polyethylene, and recently Plastrene (*see* Section 8.5). The major advantage of this constructional method is that it allows the fabrication of models of variable thickness (thermal forming techniques can only produce uniform thickness models). Shrinkage of the model material during cooling can produce cracks and cause trouble when attempting to remove model from mould so care needs to be taken in the design of the moulds and in the casting technique. The method of building layer upon layer of glass fibre cloth over a single mould and binding this with resin is described in Section 8.6.

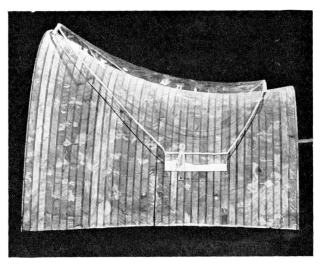

Fig. 4.15. A wooden mould made up of segments for a plastic hyperbolic paraboloid shell.

Plaster of Paris is always mixed by adding the plaster to water. It can be mixed either by hand or by a small laboratory mixer until it reaches a smooth creamy consistency. The plaster mix is poured into the mould which must be well oiled, and any air bubbles are removed by hand tamping. If linear elastic behaviour of the model is required, it must be oven cured to remove all excess moisture, and then coated with an impervious material. Moist curing, on the other hand, produces non-linear behaviour.

Micro-concretes can be cast in the same manner as cement mortars. Ideally the aggregates are scaled down according to the dimensional analysis; however, this would introduce colloidal sized particles which would alter the strength characteristics of the mix, so that a minimum aggregate size is specified. High early strength cements are used, both because they have a slightly finer grinding and because they ensure that complete gain of strength has been achieved by all parts of the model before testing occurs. Curing should continue for at least seven days under standard conditions if high early strength cement is used, and the model should be removed from the curing chamber at least 24 hours prior to testing.

4.5.5. SPIN-FORMING TECHNIQUES.—These are used in the manufacture of model shells [4.27]. A flat disc of model material is cold formed into the desired shape by spinning it at a very high rate while pressing a wooden or metal mould against it. The resulting shell is an exact replica of the geometry of the mould. This method is limited to shells derived from surfaces of revolution and also to the use of soft metals as model materials.

Chapter 5

Instrumentation of Structural Models

5.1. Model Measurements

In any structural experiment certain effects or quantities have to be measured. The most common measurements in model investigations are:

(i)   displacement
(ii) strain
(iii) force

and less frequently:

(iv) velocity
(v)   acceleration
(vi) frequency.

Instruments generally give their best performance for one particular type of measurement, and because of the increasing number available, their relative merits should be assessed for each type of model study. The most important factors pertaining to an instrument are:

(i)   sensitivity
(ii) accuracy
(iii) feedback effect
(iv) gauge length (for strain measurements).

The sensitivity of the instrument is the smallest readable unit; it must not be confused with accuracy which is a measure of reliability. Sensitivity can be increased by electrical or mechanical amplification without improving accuracy. The accuracy of a measurement denotes the degree of confidence with which it represents the true quantity.

An instrument has weight, requires a small force to activate its mechanism and may also offer a stiffening effect to the model. The weight and resistance decrease the experimental reading, and this error in the measurement is termed the feedback effect. The stiffer the model, the smaller is this error.

Displacement, strain and force measurements suffice for statical model studies, the displacement and strain being the responses of the structure to the forces applied. Dynamic loads, such as wind forces, are frequently represented by static loads in order to simplify the model construction and instrumentation. When this simplification is not justifiable, dynamic model tests must be undertaken. The need to measure time-variable quantities imposes severe demands on the measuring instruments if the rate of change of the structural responses is very fast.

The *techniques of instrumentation* of physical model analysis are divided into indirect and direct methods, depending on whether the model is subject to direct applied loading or applied displacement (according to Müller–Breslau principle, *see* Section 2.3).

A comparative summary of the various techniques of model analysis is presented in Table 5.1.

Table 5.1

Characteristics of model analysis techniques

Technique	Force	Displacement	Curvature	Strain	Point P Field F	Static S Dynamic D
Rule		★			P	S
Micrometer		★			P	S
Dial gauge		★			P	S
Level		★			P	S
Travelling microscope		★			P	S
Photogrammetric		★			P, F	S, D
Microgrids		★		★	P, F	S
Mech. strain gauge				★	P	S
Electrical strain gauge				★	P	S, D
Acoust. strain gauge				★	P	S, D
Pneumatic strain gauge				★	P	S
Photoelastic model				★	P, F	S, D
Photoelastic gauges				★	P	S
Photoelastic coating				★	P, F	S, D
Brittle coating				★	P, F	S
Moiré fringe		★		★	P, F	S, D
Curvometer			★		P	S, D
Spring balance	★				P	S
Proving ring	★				P	S
Load cell	★				P	S, D
Pressure manometer	★				P	S, D

5.2. Deflection Measurements

Static deflection measurements are commonly performed with dial gauges, graduated in 0·001 inch or 0·0001 inch. Although the force required to move the plunger of a dial gauge is small (generally of the order of 0·05 to 0·1 lb for 1 inch travel of the dial gauge) it must be taken into consideration with very flexible models, such as those used in the analysis of suspension structures. Micrometers have the advantage of not imposing a spring force on the model and an electric-eye circuit is easily devised to light up when the micrometer plunger makes contact with the model; but they can only be used for simple models because the response is not automatic. For dynamic measurements electrical transducers are preferred because of the speed of response. Survey levelling and photogrammetry [2.12] have occasionally been applied to measuring model displacements, but they suffer from lack of sensitivity and are more applicable to large models.

Rotations can be observed optically by the angle change of a reflected beam of light; usually the light is focussed onto a transparent scale with a reference image.

5.3. Strain Measurements

Since stress is not a fundamental physical quantity it cannot be measured; however, it may be determined through the relationship between stress and strain since strain can be measured.

Linear strain, ε is defined as: $\varepsilon = \lim_{L \to 0} \left(\frac{\Delta L}{L} \right)$

where L is the original length and ΔL is the change in length. In the experimental determination of strain the gauge length, L, has a finite value so that an average value of the strain over this length is measured. Because of this experimental expedient there exists the possibility of error: we have three possible cases as shown in Fig. 5.1.

5.1(a)   region of constant strain—no error
5.1(b)   region of linear strain gradient—no error
5.1(c)   region of non-linear strain gradient—error.

The error due to the non-linear part of the strain gradient as shown in Fig. 5.1(c) can be reduced by employing a smaller gauge length, *L*. This, however, presupposes no scale effects in the materials (*see* Section 4.4). Metals satisfy this condition whereas concrete, due to its composition, does not. Therefore the ideal of an infinitely short gauge length has to be modified by the necessity for the gauge length to be large compared to the maximum aggregate dimension.

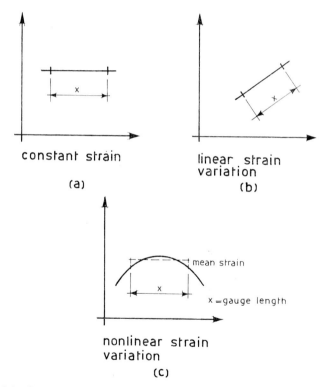

Fig. 5.1.   Sources of error in strain measurement. (a) Region of constant strain—no error, (b) region of linear strain gradient—no error, (c) region of non-linear strain gradient—error.

The ideal strain gauge may be described as one that possesses the following qualities:

(i)   small size
(ii)   negligible mass
(iii)   easily attached to the model
(iv)   extremely sensitive to strain
(v)   insensitive to extraneous environmental conditions (temperature, vibration, humidity)
(vi)   suitable for both static and dynamic measurements
(vii) suitable for remote monitoring
(viii) inexpensive
(ix)   infinitesimal gauge length
(x)   re-usable.

Table 5.2 presents a summary of the commonly used mechanical and electrical strain gauges in terms of the above specification.

Table 5.2

Characteristics of mechanical and electrical strain gauges

Characteristic	Gauge			
	Huggenberger	Demac	Electric Resistance	Semiconductor
1. Size	medium	large	very small	very small
2. Mass	small	high	negligible	negligible
3. Attachment	simple	simple	time and care	time and care
4. Sensitivity	good	moderate	excellent	excellent
5. Outside "noise"	not sensitive	not sensitive	sensitive	very sensitive
6. Dynamic	no	no	yes	yes
7. Monitoring	local	local	remote	remote
8. Cost of gauge	moderate	moderate	very low	low
9. Gauge length	$\frac{1}{2}$ in.–2 in.	6 in.–10 in.	$\frac{1}{64}$ in.–6 in.	$\frac{1}{20}$ in.–$\frac{1}{2}$ in.
10. Recovery	yes	yes	no	no

The Huggenberger tensometer [5.1, 5.2] is one of the best mechanical strain gauges. It has a magnification of up to 2,000 and gauge lengths of $\frac{1}{2}$ inch and 1 inch (Fig. 5.2); a recent model has a gauge length of 0·2 inch and a magnification of 3,000. It is sufficiently robust to withstand handling. Although it is comparatively light, attachment, by means of special clamps, springs or elastic bands, becomes difficult for complex models. It can measure strains as low as 1×10^{-5}.

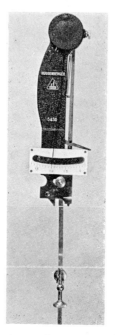

Fig. 5.2.   The Huggenberger tensometer: a comparatively light, robust mechanical strain gauge capable of measuring strains of 1×10^{-5}.

Long-gauge-length mechanical tensometers (2 inch to 10 inch) [5.3, 5.4] reduce the need for high magnification. A dial gauge reading to 0·0001 inch is usually employed; greater sensitivity is obtained by means of simple levers. Examples of this type of gauge are the *Tensotest*, made by Huggenberger, and the *Demac* gauge, developed by the Cement and Concrete Association, England [5.5]. These tensometers are particularly suitable for testing large models where the long gauge length is acceptable.

   There are three main sources of error when using mechanical strain gauges:

(i) errors inherent in the instrument itself. These can arise from inaccuracies in the construction of the mechanism; from a loss of motion in the gears (back lash); from the effects of temperature changes on the parts of the gauge, and from a deformation of the parts of the gauge by the forces needed to operate it.

(ii) errors caused by the method used to mount the gauge on the model. These can arise from the forces used to press the gauge against the model (contact pressure); from the distortion of the model itself by the gauge mounting force, and from the location of the measuring points with respect to the surface of the model.

(iii) errors arising from the use of the gauge itself. These include parallax errors in reading scales, and disturbance of the gauge by vibration or accidental contact.

Optical strain gauges are similar to mechanical strain gauges in having one end fixed and the other end moving by rotation. The chief difference between the two gauges is in the lever system; the optical gauge uses light rays instead of mechanical levers. This eliminates the inertia of the magnification system. The most widely used optical strain gauge is the *Tuckerman gauge* [5.6, 5.7] which has a sensitivity of 2 microstrain,* but its main drawback is the skill required to operate it and the difficulty of mounting it on the model.

The acoustical or vibrating-wire strain gauge [5.8, 5.9] dates back to the late 1920's. Its operating principle is based on the fact that a stretched wire, when plucked, vibrates at a particular frequency (resonant frequency) which depends on the tension in that wire.

$$f = \frac{1}{2L} \sqrt{\frac{T}{\rho}} \qquad (5.1)$$

where f is the frequency of vibration, L is the length of wire, ρ is the material density and T is the wire tension. Also,

$$T = AE\varepsilon \qquad (5.2)$$

where A is the cross-sectional area of the wire, E is the elastic modulus of the wire and ε is the strain in the wire.

---

* One microstrain = strain of 1×10^{-6}.

Substituting eqn. (5.2) into (5.1)

$$\varepsilon = \frac{4\,\rho L^2}{EA}\cdot f^2. \tag{5.3}$$

Let us assume that the natural frequency of a test wire, stretched between two fixed points on the model and made to vibrate, is f_0. Straining the model stretches the wire further, so that the frequency of vibration becomes f_1; the change in the strain of the wire, given by eqn. (5.3), is then

$$\Delta\varepsilon = \varepsilon_1 - \varepsilon_0 = \frac{4\,\rho L^2}{EA}\cdot(f_1{}^2 - f_0{}^2).$$

Jerrett has given a detailed description of the acoustic strain gauge [5.10]. It is suitable for applications requiring long-term stability and high sensitivity. Its main disadvantage is its bulk and stiffness, which makes it unsuitable for strain measurements on flexible models. However, it is sufficiently robust to be cast into concrete members for measuring strains at interior points in the prototype.

Electrical resistance strain gauges utilize one of the following physical effects:

(i)   change in capacitance
(ii) change in inductance
(iii) change in resistance
(iv) the piezoelectric effect.

The *capacitance strain gauge* [5.11] utilizes the principle that the capacitance of a parallel plate condenser is changed by varying the separation of the plates or the surface area common to both plates. Whilst this gauge is not normally used with architectural models, it is employed where high temperatures are necessary.

The *inductance strain gauge* [5.12, 5.13] utilizes the electrical induction effect of a moving magnetic core within an electric coil. The *linear differential transformer* [5.14] is a device for converting mechanical displacements into electrical signals. It can be employed in a large variety of transducer applications, not only for strain, but also for displacement, pressure, acceleration, force and temperature. The main advantage of the inductance strain gauge is its high stability, high energy of output signal, high sensitivity and robust construction. Its use has been limited because of the difficulty of mechanical attachment, a problem common to all gauges except the bonded resistance gauges.

The *electrical resistance strain gauge* utilizes the principle, discovered by Lord Kelvin in 1856 [5.15], that the resistance of iron and copper increases with increased tensile strain. He also established that the resistance of a wire changes as a function of strain; that different materials have different sensitivities; and that the Wheatstone bridge can be employed to measure accurately these resistance changes. However, wire resistance strain gauges became commercially available only in the 1940's. There are four main classes of resistance strain gauges:

   (i)   unbonded-wire gauges
   (ii) bonded-wire gauges
  (iii) bonded-foil gauges
  (iv) semi-conductor (piezoresistive) gauges.

The resistance, R, of a wire of cross-sectional area A, length L, and specific resistance ρ is given by the equation

$$R = \rho \frac{L}{A}.$$

It can be shown that [5.16]

$$\frac{dR}{R} = \frac{d\rho}{\rho} + \frac{dL}{L}(1 + 2\mu)$$

where μ is Poisson's ratio of the wire. Therefore

$$\frac{dR}{R} \bigg/ \frac{dL}{L} = (1 + 2\mu) + \frac{d\rho}{\rho} \bigg/ \frac{dL}{L}.$$

The ratio $\dfrac{dR}{R} \bigg/ \dfrac{dL}{L}$, called the *gauge factor* (G.F.), measures the gauge sensitivity. A high gauge factor is desirable to reduce the necessary amplification.

A copper–nickel alloy, *Advance*, is commonly used as the wire or foil material. It has:

   (i)   a large linear range
   (ii) a G.F. that remains constant in the plastic range
   (iii) a high ρ, so that a small grid is possible
   (iv) a relatively low temperature coefficient.

Unbonded-wire strain gauges [5.16] are rarely used in direct stress analysis since they are more cumbersome to use than bonded-wire and bonded-foil gauges, and are greatly affected by temperature variations. However, they are useful for measuring strains in model prestressing wires.

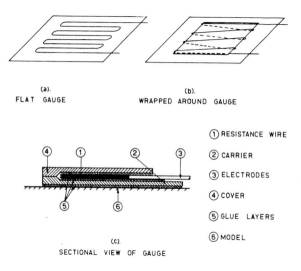

          (a).   (b).
    FLAT GAUGE   WRAPPED AROUND GAUGE

① RESISTANCE WIRE
② CARRIER
③ ELECTRODES
④ COVER
⑤ GLUE LAYERS
⑥ MODEL

(c).
SECTIONAL VIEW OF GAUGE

Fig. 5.3.   Bonded-wire strain gauges. (a) Wound, flat strain gauge, (b) wrapped-around strain gauge, (c) cross-section of bonded-wire strain gauge.

Bonded-wire strain gauges [5.17, 5.18, 5.19] consist of a continuous length of resistance wire approximately 0·001 inch in diameter, wound to form a flat gauge as in Fig. 5.3(a) or a wrapped-around gauge as in Fig. 5.3(b). The grid is sandwiched between two sheets of paper or other backing material, to facilitate handling and provide electrical insulation. A cross-section of a bonded-wire strain gauge is shown in Fig. 5.3(c).

Bonded-foil strain gauges [5.20] are based on the same principle as bonded-wire gauges. A metal foil, 0·0001 inch to 0·0004 inch thick (0·0025 mm to 0·01 mm), is used in the fabrication of the grid, which is photo-etched into the desired shape. Because of this refinement several important advantages accrue:

(i)   the thinner element permits a reduction in gauge length to $\frac{1}{64}$ inch (approximately 0·4 mm)
(ii)   since the foil element is many times wider than it is thick, it provides a greater area for bonding and for heat dissipation
(iii) thinness of the gauge decreases the stiffening effect on flexible models.

Because of the importance of the electrical resistance strain gauge, it will be discussed more fully in the next section.

Semi-conductor or piezo-resistive strain gauges are based on the piezo-resistive phenomenon observed in 1954 by Smith [5.21]; in 1957 this was applied to measure displacement and forces [5.22]. No attempt will be made to describe the physical behaviour of the semi-conductor since it requires a knowledge of solid-state physics which is beyond the scope of this book. The semi-conductor gauge has a gauge factor of up to 250 compared with approximately 2 for conventional wire or foil gauges. It has excellent stability; at constant temperature it is virtually creep- and hysteresis-free. However, it has a limited linear range and is very sensitive to temperature variations. Whilst foil gauges may in time replace wire gauges, the expensive semi-conductor gauges are likely to be confined to special applications in which the high sensitivity is desirable, *e.g.* special pressure transducers for foundation studies.

Other special electrical resistance strain gauges are now available. One is the weldable strain gauge developed for use at elevated temperatures. It consists of a fine resistance element swaged onto a metal base with compacted magnesium oxide as an insulator and is suitable for a temperature range of -390 to $+750°F$ (-230 to $+400°C$).

In the *self-adhesive strain gauge*, recently developed at the Royal Aircraft Establishment, England [5.23] but not yet commercially available, the resistance element is a metallic coating, vacuum-deposited onto a thin polyester strip, which is heat-sealed between two small pieces of elastomer. Self-adhesion is provided by the bond between the plate-polished surfaces of the low-modulus elastomer (*e.g.* plasticised polyvinyl chloride) and the harder model surface (*e.g.* Perspex, steel, etc.). This bond has sufficiently high shear strength, but does not resist peeling; hence a self-adhesive gauge which is thin and flexible can be repeatedly fixed to a specimen to explore the strain field.

The *pneumatic strain gauge* developed in the late 1930's [5.24, 5.25], has been successfully employed to overcome the difficulties of mechanical magnification. The development of the electrical strain gauges a few years later overshadowed its potential. However, in recent years it has been used to measure strains in models and structures which are subject to radiant heat fields and rapid changes in temperature, since its construction avoids differential expansion between it and the model.

5.4. Electrical Resistance Strain Gauges

Since the electrical bonded-wire or foil resistance strain gauge is the one most commonly used in model measurements, its operation is considered in detail in this section.

The strain sensing element is glued to a *carrier* or backing material to facilitate handling. Three are commonly used:

(i) *Paper* as backing material allows production of a relatively cheap gauge. It is satisfactory for short term tests only, because of drift. Thin paper is sometimes used to permit shorter glue drying schedules and improve gauge flexibility. It is harder to handle than the more commonly used thicker material because the wire can be forced through the backing.

(ii) *Phenolic impregnated paper* is used as backing material when high temperatures are to be expected. It can be employed in temperatures up to 400°F (200°C) for static tests and up to 800°F for dynamic tests; it has negligible creep or hysteresis.

(iii) *Epoxy resin* is the usual backing material for foil gauges. It can be employed in temperatures up to 200°F (95°C) with negligible creep and hysteresis.

The element of the gauge responsible for many of its physical characteristics is the *adhesive*—both that used in the gauge construction and for attachment; the same adhesive may be used for both. While there is a variety of adhesives, five are commonly used:

(i) *Cellulose-based adhesives, e.g.* cellulose nitrate, set by solvent release over a wide range of temperature and time, depending on application the drying time at room temperature may vary from two to ten days. This may be shortened by using higher temperatures, say over 100°F (38°C). As up to 80 per cent of the adhesive may evaporate, a path must be left for the exit of the solvent; hence hot air heating is preferred to radiant heating. The adhesive is characterized by a high strain limit (over 10 per cent) and a high rate of water absorption.

(ii) *Phenolic resins* polymerise under the action of heat and pressure; their curing temperature varies from 250 to 350°F (120 to 170°C) with pressures of about 100 lb/sq inch. For best results it is necessary to leave a path for the solvent and water vapor; curing time is about 6 hours. To avoid time dependent zero shifts, a post-curing cycle is recommended.

(iii) *Epoxy resins* are of two types—those which set by chemical action at ambient temperature and those requiring heat curing. Both are two-component types, the hardener and the resin being mixed just prior to use. Since there is no volume change during curing, there is no necessity for post-curing. The pressure during curing need be little more than that needed to hold the gauge in place.

(iv) *Cyanoacrylate resin* (*Eastman 910*) is a pressure-sensitive adhesive which polymerises almost instantaneously at room temperature in the presence of pressure. Like the epoxy resins, there is no volume change during polymerisation and hence no need for post-curing. Service temperature is about 200°F (95°C).

(v) *Ceramic materials* are used where high service temperatures are required. There is a variety of such adhesives which are characterized by comparatively low strain limits; they require high temperature curing and are frequently hygroscopic.

All gauge adhesives have a limited shelf life and are best kept under refrigeration. This applies even to those adhesives having two components; the shelf life varies from 3 to 18 months and makers' recommendations in this matter should be carefully followed, for it is generally not possible to detect easily when shelf life has been exceeded.

Not all gauge adhesive combinations are possible. It is clearly unsatisfactory to use an adhesive with a cure temperature higher than the operating temperature of the gauge. Paper gauges are used with cellulose-nitrate adhesive, room-temperature-cure epoxy resins, or any rapid-set adhesive; Eastman 910 is satisfactory if used with a special catalyst. Phenolic-based gauges are used with phenolic resin, Eastman 910 or epoxy resins, but not the rapid-set adhesives. Epoxy-base gauges are used with epoxy resin, Eastman 910, but not cellulose-based adhesives.

Since the condition of the adhesive bonding of the gauge to the model materially influences the behaviour of the gauge, it is advisable that each gauge be inspected prior to use to determine the adequacy of the bond. No tests must be undertaken before the gauge and the cement are absolutely dry and cured. A visual check may suffice to determine whether there are air-pockets in the cement between the gauge and the model. A rough measurement can also be made by connecting a meter across the gauge since, by gently pressing the gauge with a piece of soft material, the meter shows a reading equivalent to several micro-strain if air-pockets are present. If air-pockets exist, it is advisable to remove the strain gauge and start again. The resistance value of the gauge has to be checked by means of an ohm-meter, since during cementing the wire may be broken or there may be an open circuit in the connection cable. The insulation resistance between the gauge grid and the model may be measured by means of a megohm-meter. This resistance has to be higher than 600 megohms; gauges with a resistance lower than 600 megohms, but higher than 100 megohms, can be used for rough short-term measurements. Below 100 megohms the gauge should be replaced; if moisture-proofing has not been applied, preheating with infrared lamps for some hours may result in an increased resistance value.

Moisture plays an important role in the measuring accuracy of the strain gauge. It can produce dimensional changes in the cement between the gauge and the model, resulting in apparent strains. Furthermore, the resistance of the gauge may change due to the extra conductivity of the absorbed moisture. Paper gauges are sensitive to moisture; phenolic gauges are less affected. Paper gauges can be moisture-proofed by a covering layer of grease, wax or silicone; but care must be taken that the gauge and cement are absolutely dry.

The *Wheatstone bridge* circuit is commonly used for measuring the change of resistance in the gauge element produced by straining. Of the four arms of the bridge, two are occupied by standard resistors, the third is occupied by the *active gauge* and the fourth by the *dummy gauge*. This configuration, shown in Fig. 5.4 is termed a half-bridge. The object of the dummy gauge is to eliminate any unbalance of the bridge arising either from self-heating of the active gauge or from changes in the ambient temperature. Since the dummy gauge should be subjected to the same environment as the active gauge, it is ideally mounted on material identical to the model material.

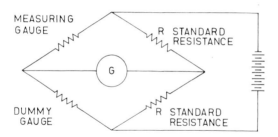

Fig. 5.4. The Wheatstone bridge circuit used in strain measuring circuits. The *dummy* gauge is used to eliminate imbalance due to change in temperature.

A more flexible method of measurement, using the Wheatstone bridge, is called the *direct reading* or deflection method; this utilizes the bridge network shown in Fig. 5.4 the galvanometer of which can be calibrated for direct reading in micro-strain units by a suitable scale multiplier. The direct reading method can be used for both static and dynamic measurements because of the high speed of response of the total system. When only static measurements are required the *null balance method* is employed. It is generally more accurate than the direct reading bridge circuit, but the time taken to re-balance precludes its use for dynamic measurements. A potentiometer, called the apex resistance, is added between the standard resistances of the direct reading bridge circuit (Fig. 5.4), and the galvanometer is tapped into it. By adjusting this resistor through an accurately measured amount, directly converted to micro-strain, the galvanometer needle is brought back to zero and the bridge re-balanced.

Thermal stability of the gauge is particularly important if comparative readings are to be taken in a test run extending over a significant period of time. An increase in ambient temperature gives rise to:

(i)   an increase in gauge resistance $\dfrac{\Delta R}{R} = \eta . \Delta T$

(ii) an elongation of the gauge grid $\dfrac{\Delta L}{L} = \alpha . \Delta T$

$$\text{or } \frac{\Delta R}{R} = \alpha . \Delta T . \text{GF}$$

(iii) an elongation of the gauge mounting material

$$\frac{\Delta L}{L} = \beta . \Delta T$$

$$\text{or } \frac{\Delta R}{R} = \beta . \Delta T . \ \text{GF}$$

where α is the thermal coefficient of expansion of the gauge material, β is the thermal coefficient expansion of the base material, η is the temperature coefficient of resistivity of the gauge material, and GF is the gauge factor.

The combined effect of these three factors produces a temperature-induced change in the resistance of the gauge:

$$\frac{\Delta R}{R} = (\beta - \alpha) \Delta T . \text{GF} + \eta . \Delta T. \tag{5.4}$$

When $\beta \neq \alpha$, there is a differential expansion between the gauge and the base material due to temperature change and the gauge is subjected to a mechanical strain of $\varepsilon = (\beta - \alpha) \Delta T$, which does not occur in the model. It is impossible to separate this apparent strain due to temperature from a strain due to the applied load.

If the gauge material and the base material have identical coefficients of expansion, the first component of $\Delta R/R$ in eqn. (5.4) vanishes. However, if the coefficient of resistivity $\eta \neq 0$ an apparent strain, impossible to separate from the load-induced strain, may be indicated, which is proportional to the temperature change. Temperature-compensated gauges, manufactured from materials which reduce the net effect of the factors in eqn. (5.4) to zero, are expensive and tend to have a non-linear response. It is therefore customary to use a dummy gauge in the bridge circuit, as in Fig. 5.4 [5.26].

Resistance of leads in strain gauge circuits should be kept low to avoid dead resistance in series with the gauge. For an inserted resistance of 1 ohm, the gauge factor of a 120 ohm gauge is reduced by nearly 1 per cent. More serious is the resistance change arising from temperature differences in the leads. This can be brought about by heating from an external source (such as direct sunlight) or by self-heating from the gauge current, or from different temperature coefficients of the leads. For example, for a 120 ohm gauge with a gauge factor of 2, the actual change in resistance for a strain of 0·001 is 0·24 ohms; allowing a lead resistance of 1 ohm in copper (which has a temperature coefficient of resistivity of 0·004 per °C), an error of about 2 per cent results for a temperature change in the lead of 1°C. In general, for leads of less than twenty feet, lead resistance need not be taken into account for the ensuing error is less than the error of the total measuring system. The use of thicker wires reduces lead resistance, but these wires are so heavy that special precautions must be taken to prevent them breaking the gauge connection wire.

The very high resistance of the gauge element generates heat. When the model is made of a poor thermal conductor, such as plastic, heat dissipation is slow; about fifteen minutes must be allowed after switching on the current for the gauge to reach thermal equilibrium. Pre-heating of the guages, using an ancillary circuit, is recommended to bring all gauges close to thermal equilibrium. Pre-heating is essential for high frequency automatic switching and reading.

To measure biaxial states of strain at a point we need three gauges (*see* Section 5.5). There are a number of commercially manufactured *rosettes* of three gauges on one backing piece (Fig. 5.5).

Since strain gauges measure strain only at one point on a model, a large number of gauges must be used if whole-field coverage is needed. To reduce the time required to read and record these gauges, switching units automatically connect, consecutively, a number of gauges to the strain bridge; by utilising the same dummy gauge for a

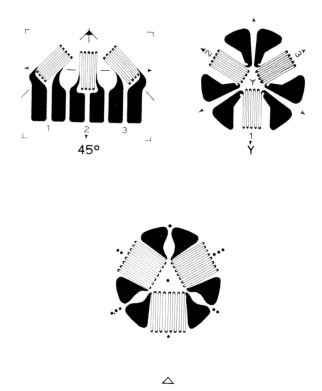

Fig. 5.5. Strain gauge rosettes: 45°, "Y" and Δ shaped; used to measure biaxial states of stress.

number of active gauges, the number of gauges is reduced by almost half. Many such units, *e.g.* the Philips switching unit PT1210–1211, contain pre-heating circuits for each active gauge which allows high frequency automatic switching of up to 10 gauge-channels per second without loss of accuracy. Automatic switching considerably extends the usefulness of switching equipment, but necessitates the use of automatic recording devices. The automatic switching and recording strain gauge system shown in Fig. 5.6 consists of two batteries of ten-channel automatic switching units with inbuilt pre-heating circuits coupled, through a direct reading bridge, to a digital voltmeter for visual display. The digital voltmeter serialises the output from the bridge for the two methods of automatic recording used: a solenoid-driven electric typewriter for an immediate and permanent visual record and a paper tape perforator which outputs the

Fig. 5.6. An automatic switching and recording strain gauge system which consists of two batteries of ten-channel automatic switching units coupled, through a direct reading bridge, to a digital voltmeter and an automatic electric typewriter. (*Architectural Science Laboratory, University of Sydney.*)

results in the form of a five-channel paper tape. This tape can then be used as the data tape for a computer program to calculate the principal stresses from the readings, carry out a statistical analysis of the results, and plot them on a graph [5.27]. It is a simple matter to produce a further program which converts the strains on the data tape to prototype moments and forces.

5.5. Interpretation of Strain Gauge Results

It can be shown [5.28] that in any state of combined stress a cubic element can be cut in such a manner as to have only normal stresses (tension or compression) on its six sides. These stresses are by definition the *principal stresses*; the strains on the same planes are the *principal strains*. To ascertain stress conditions it is necessary to determine the magnitude and direction of the principal stresses at a sufficient number of points to cover the field adequately. As strain gauges determine surface stresses only, we shall limit ourselves to a two-dimensional stress system. Since three strains at a point completely define the state of stress at that point, strain rosettes are used. Alternatively we can measure ε_1 and ε_2, the two principal strains, and the direction, θ, of one of them with respect to some previously defined axis. Conversion of strains to stresses requires a knowledge of the elastic modulus, E, and Poisson's ratio, μ.

In the simplest case of uniaxial stress, a single strain gauge is sufficient to define the stress field. If ε is the strain measured in the direction parallel to the stress, σ, then

$$\sigma = E.\varepsilon.$$

In most cases the directions of the principal stresses are not known. In a two-dimensional stress field, there are three strains, the normal strains ε_x and ε_y parallel to the x- and y-axes, and the shear strain γ_{xy}. A strain, ε_θ, measured in an arbitrary direction at an angle θ to the x-axis is then given by

$$\varepsilon_\theta = \tfrac{1}{2}(\varepsilon_x + \varepsilon_y) + \tfrac{1}{2}(\varepsilon_x - \varepsilon_y)\cos 2\theta + \tfrac{1}{2}\gamma_{xy}\sin 2\theta. \qquad (5.5)$$

The values of ε_x, ε_y and γ_{xy} may be determined by picking three arbitrary directions, θ_a, θ_b and θ_c, and solving the three resultant simultaneous equations. The principal strains and principal directions correspond to the maximum and minimum values of ε_θ, so that on differentiating equation (5.5) and equating the result to zero the directions of the principal strains ε_1 and ε_2 are

$$\theta = \tfrac{1}{2}\tan^{-1}\left[\frac{\gamma_{xy}}{\varepsilon_x - \varepsilon_y}\right] \qquad (5.6)$$

where θ is the angle between the principal axis and the x-axis. Substituting eqn. (5.6) into eqn. (5.5) yields the principal strains

$$\varepsilon_1 = \tfrac{1}{2}(\varepsilon_x + \varepsilon_y) + \tfrac{1}{2}\sqrt{(\varepsilon_x - \varepsilon_y)^2 + \gamma_{xy}{}^2}$$

$$\varepsilon_2 = \tfrac{1}{2}(\varepsilon_x + \varepsilon_y) - \tfrac{1}{2}\sqrt{(\varepsilon_x - \varepsilon_y)^2 + \gamma_{xy}{}^2}. \qquad (5.7)$$

In practice, rosettes with three gauges set at fixed angles are used, either a 45° rectangular rosette, or a 120° Y rosette, or a 120° Δ rosette; the configuration of these is shown in Fig. 5.5.

For the *45° rectangular rosette*, using eqn. (5.5)

$$\varepsilon_0 = \varepsilon_x$$
$$\varepsilon_{45} = \tfrac{1}{2}(\varepsilon_x + \varepsilon_y + \gamma_{xy}) \qquad (5.8)$$
$$\varepsilon_{90} = \varepsilon_y.$$

The principal strains ε_1 and ε_2 are then obtained by substituting the values of ε_x, ε_y and γ_{xy} derived from eqn. (5.8) into eqn. (5.7), giving

$$\varepsilon_1 = \tfrac{1}{2}(\varepsilon_0 + \varepsilon_{90}) + \tfrac{1}{2}\sqrt{(\varepsilon_0 - \varepsilon_{90})^2 + (2\varepsilon_{45} - \varepsilon_0 - \varepsilon_{90})^2}$$

$$\varepsilon_2 = \tfrac{1}{2}(\varepsilon_0 + \varepsilon_{90}) - \tfrac{1}{2}\sqrt{(\varepsilon_0 - \varepsilon_{90})^2 + (2\varepsilon_{45} - \varepsilon_0 - \varepsilon_{90})^2}$$

and the principal angle θ is given by

$$\theta = \tfrac{1}{2}\tan^{-1}\left|\frac{2\varepsilon_{45} - \varepsilon_0 - \varepsilon_{90}}{\varepsilon_0 - \varepsilon_{90}}\right|.$$

This gives two values of θ corresponding to the directions of ε_1 and ε_2.

For the *120° Y rosette* and the *120° Δ rosette*, using eqn. (5.5)

$$\varepsilon_0 = \varepsilon_x$$

$$\varepsilon_{120} = \tfrac{1}{4}\varepsilon_x + \tfrac{3}{4}\varepsilon_y - \frac{\sqrt{3}}{4}\gamma_{xy} \qquad (5.9)$$

$$\varepsilon_{240} = \tfrac{1}{4}\varepsilon_x + \tfrac{3}{4}\varepsilon_y + \frac{\sqrt{3}}{4}\gamma_{xy}.$$

The principal strains ε_1 and ε_2 are then obtained by substituting the values of ε_x, ε_y and γ_{xy} derived from eqn. (5.9) into eqn. (5.7), giving

$$\varepsilon_1 = \tfrac{1}{3}(\varepsilon_0 + \varepsilon_{120} + \varepsilon_{240}) + \sqrt{[\varepsilon_0 - \tfrac{1}{3}(\varepsilon_0 + \varepsilon_{120} + \varepsilon_{240})]^2 + \tfrac{1}{3}(\varepsilon_{120} - \varepsilon_{240})^2}$$

$$\varepsilon_2 = \tfrac{1}{3}(\varepsilon_0 + \varepsilon_{120} + \varepsilon_{240}) - \sqrt{[\varepsilon_0 - \tfrac{1}{3}(\varepsilon_0 + \varepsilon_{120} + \varepsilon_{240})]^2 + \tfrac{1}{3}(\varepsilon_{120} - \varepsilon_{240})^2}$$

and the principal angle θ is given by

$$\theta = \tfrac{1}{2}\tan^{-1}\left\{\frac{1/\sqrt{3}\,(\varepsilon_{240} - \varepsilon_{120})}{\varepsilon_0 - \tfrac{1}{3}(\varepsilon_0 + \varepsilon_{120} + \varepsilon_{240})}\right\}.$$

Having calculated the principal strains ε_1 and ε_2, the principal stresses are then given by

$$\sigma_1 = \frac{E}{1 - \mu^2} (\varepsilon_1 + \mu\varepsilon_2)$$

(5.10)

$$\sigma_2 = \frac{E}{1 - \mu^2} (\varepsilon_2 + \mu\varepsilon_1)$$

and the maximum shear stress, inclined at 45° to the principal axis, is given by

$$\tau_{max} = \frac{E}{2(1 + \mu)} \gamma_{max}$$

where

$$\gamma_{max} = 2(\varepsilon_1 - \varepsilon_2).$$

A number of methods have been developed [5.29, 5.30, 5.31, 5.32] to expedite the evaluation of principal stresses from strain rosette readings; they include graphical methods such as the Mohr's circle, nomographs, special strain gauge computers, as well as digital computer programs similar to those described in Section 5.4.

When *shells* are analysed with models, the magnitude and distribution of the total forces N_x, N_y, N_{xy} and moments M_x, M_y, M_{xy} are determined from strain gauge readings. It can be shown [5.33] that

$$N_x = \frac{Et}{1 - \mu^2} \left(\frac{\partial u}{\partial x} + \mu\frac{\partial v}{\partial y} \right)$$

$$N_y = \frac{Et}{1 - \mu^2} \left(\frac{\partial v}{\partial y} + \mu\frac{\partial u}{\partial x} \right)$$

$$N_{yx} = N_{xy} = \frac{Et}{2(1 + \mu)} \left(\frac{\partial u}{\partial y} + \frac{\partial v}{\partial x} \right)$$

and

(5.11)

$$M_x = -\frac{Et^3}{12(1 - \mu^2)} \left(\frac{\partial^2 w}{\partial x^2} + \mu\frac{\partial^2 w}{\partial y^2} \right)$$

$$M_y = -\frac{Et^3}{12(1 - \mu^2)} \left(\frac{\partial^2 w}{\partial y^2} + \mu\frac{\partial^2 w}{\partial x^2} \right)$$

$$M_{xy} = -M_{yx} = \frac{Et^3}{12(1 + \mu)} \cdot \frac{\partial^2 w}{\partial x \partial y}$$

where t is the shell thickness, u is the displacement of middle surface in the x direction, v is the displacement of the middle surface in the y direction, w is the displacement of the middle surface in the z direction, E is the elastic modulus, and μ is Poisson's ratio. The surface strain ε_x at a distance $t/2$ from the middle surface is made up of two strain components: an axial strain component, ε_{x0}, and a strain component due to bending, $t/2 \cdot \chi_x$, where χ_x is the change in curvature, *i.e.*

$$\varepsilon_x = \varepsilon_{x0} \pm t/2 \cdot \chi_x$$

$$\varepsilon_y = \varepsilon_{y0} \pm t/2 \cdot \chi_y \qquad (5.12)$$

$$\gamma_{xy} = \gamma_{xy0} \pm t \cdot \chi_{xy}.$$

The values of ε_x, ε_y and γ_{xy} may be determined from eqn. (5.5) or from a rosette analysis, and the values of ε_{x0}, ε_{y0} and γ_{xy0} can be determined from eqn. (5.12). It can be shown that:

$$\frac{\partial u}{\partial x} = \varepsilon_{x0}$$

$$\frac{\partial u}{\partial y} = \varepsilon_{y0}$$

$$\frac{\partial u}{\partial y} + \frac{\partial v}{\partial x} = \gamma_{xy0}$$

$$(5.13)$$

$$\frac{\partial^2 w}{\partial x^2} = \chi_x$$

$$\frac{\partial^2 w}{\partial y^2} = \chi_y$$

$$\frac{\partial^2 w}{\partial x \delta y} = \chi_{xy}.$$

Substituting eqn. (5.13) into eqn. (5.11) we get the stress–strain relationships for membrane forces, and for bending and twisting moments

$$N_x = \frac{Et}{1 - \mu^2} (\varepsilon_{x0} + \mu \, \varepsilon_{y0})$$

$$N_y = \frac{Et}{1 - \mu^2} (\varepsilon_{y0} + \mu \, \varepsilon_{x0})$$

$$N_{xy} = \frac{Et}{2(1 + \mu)} \gamma_{xy0}$$

and   (5.14)

$$M_x = -\frac{Et^3}{12(1 - \mu^2)} (\chi_x + \mu\chi_y)$$

$$M_y = -\frac{Et^3}{12(1 - \mu^2)} (\chi_y + \mu\chi_x)$$

$$M_{xy} = \frac{Et^3}{12(1 + \mu)} \chi_{xy}.$$

5.6. Photoelastic Coating

In this technique birefringent plastic is bonded to the surface of the model. When the model is loaded, strain is conveyed to the coating. Isoclinic and isochromatic fringe patterns* appear when the coating is viewed through a reflection polariscope. The coating can be applied to the surface of the model either by applying a liquid birefringent plastic to the surface and polymerising it with heat, or by cementing sheets of birefringent plastic directly to the surface. The former method can be used on sharply curving surfaces. To obtain the reflective surface necessary on the model, reflective paint is applied or reflective cement is used for bonding. A good polished metallic surface is an adequate reflector. As discussed in Section 2.7, photoelastic coating techniques have two distinct advantages over conventional two-dimensional photoelastic techniques: they can be used on non-planar surfaces and they permit the determination of

---

* An isoclinic is the locus of points along which principal stresses have parallel directions; an isochromatic is the locus of points which have the same principal stress difference.

surface strains of a model made from any material, not just transparent plastic [5.34, 5.35]. Hawkes and Holister [5.36] give a particularly good introduction to the photoelastic coating technique.

The optical theory for photoelastic coatings is similar to that for
two-dimensional photoelasticity, except that the effective thickness
is doubled since the light passes through the coating twice. The
principles of basic photoelasticity are well known [B.6, B.7]. When a
beam of polarised light, *i.e.* one which has travelled through a
polarising sheet, passes through a birefringent material, the two
components emerging are polarised in the planes of the principal
stresses in the material. They are retarded in relation to one another
by a phase difference, which is proportional to the difference in
magnitude between the principal strains and the length of the light
path through the material.

This relationship is given by

$$r = C_\varepsilon \, l \, (\varepsilon_1 - \varepsilon_2) \tag{5.15}$$

where r is the relative retardation, C_ε is the strain optical coefficient,
and l is the length of light path. The relative retardation is measured
by the interference fringes produced when the emergent light is
viewed through a polarising sheet, called the analyser. Depending
upon the orientation of the polariser and the analyser, the condition
for the production of an isochromatic fringe of order n due to
extinction of light of wavelength λ is given by

$$r = 0$$

or $$r = n\lambda. \tag{5.16}$$

By identifying the fringe order for a given wave length of light,
the shear strain at any point is determined directly. Individual
principal strains can also be measured by this technique. Where one
of the directions of the principal strain coincides with the direction
of polarisation, the light passes through the material without being
affected. If the analyser is set at right angles to the polariser, light of
all wavelengths is extinguished and all such areas appear black;
these are isoclinics. They enable the direction of the principal strains,
and hence stresses, to be determined at any point. To enable isochromatics to be studied without interference from the isoclinics, a
removable quarter wave plate is incorporated in both the polariser

and analyser. This is a plate of crystal, the thickness of which is such as to retard one of the two rays of light passing through it by one quarter of a wavelength relative to the other, producing circularly polarised light. As there are no specific directions of polarisation, the isoclinics are eliminated in the field of view. Monochromatic light must be used, since any one set of plates are true quarter wave plates for only one particular wavelength. Figure 5.7 shows diagrammatically the principle reflection polariscope used with photoelastic

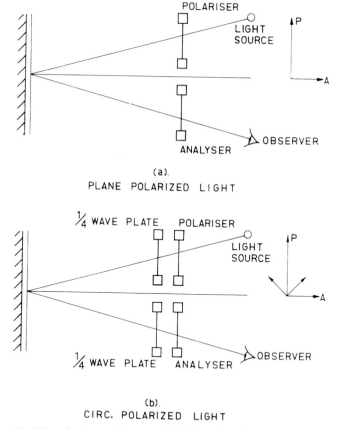

(a).
PLANE POLARIZED LIGHT

(b).
CIRC. POLARIZED LIGHT

Fig. 5.7. The reflection polariscope. (a) Viewing isoclinics using plane polarised light, (b) viewing isochromatics using circularly polarised light.

coatings; Fig. 5.7(a) shows the polariscope set up to view the isoclinics, using plane polarised light, whilst Fig. 5.7(b) shows it set up
to view isochromatics using circularly polarised light. Commercially
produced reflection polariscopes fall into two groups: large-field
reflection polariscopes which can be most effectively used on relatively flat surfaces, and small-field reflection polariscopes which can
be used on sharply curving surfaces or for investigation of small
areas containing stress concentrations.

For *photoelastic coatings* eqn. (5.15) relating the relative retardation to the shear strain becomes

$$r = C_\varepsilon\, 2t(\varepsilon_1 - \varepsilon_2)_c$$

where t is the coating thickness and the subscript c refers to the
coating. If the coating is constrained to follow exactly the deformation of the model to which it is bonded

$$(\varepsilon_1 - \varepsilon_2)_c = (\varepsilon_1 - \varepsilon_2)_m$$

i.e.
$$(\varepsilon_1 - \varepsilon_2)_m = \frac{r}{2t . C_\varepsilon}.$$

The difference between the principal stresses can now be determined
using eqn. (5.10),

$$(\sigma_1 - \sigma_2)_m = \frac{r . E_m}{2t . C_\varepsilon (1 + \mu_m)}. \qquad (5.17)$$

Eqn. (5.17) may be re-written in a form similar to that of eqn. (5.15):

$$(\sigma_1 - \sigma_2)_m = \frac{r}{2t . C_\sigma} \qquad (5.18)$$

where C_σ, the stress optical coefficient, is equal to

$$\frac{E}{1 + \mu} . C_\varepsilon.$$

From $(\sigma_1 - \sigma_2)$ and the directions of σ_1 and σ_2, the separate
principal stresses can be evaluated by the *oblique incident method*,
using the optical arrangement shown in Fig. 5.8 [5.37, 5.38]. Let us, in
eqn. (5.18), measure r in terms of multiples of the wavelength of the
light used, and replace the stress optical coefficient, C_σ, by the material

fringe value, f (defined as the stress necessary to produce a first order fringe in a plate one inch thick). Eqn. (5.18) can then be written in the form

$$r = \frac{2t}{f} (\sigma_1 - \sigma_2) \qquad (5.19)$$

where r is called the fringe order. If we now define r_1 and r_2 as

$$r_1 = \frac{2t}{f} (\sigma_1)$$

$$r_2 = \frac{2t}{f} (\sigma_2) \qquad (5.20)$$

then, by substituting eqn. (5.20) into eqn. (5.19)

$$r = r_1 - r_2. \qquad (5.21)$$

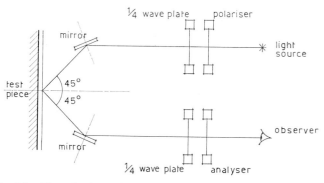

Fig. 5.8.   The reflection polariscope set up for the *oblique incident method.*

If the model is rotated about the principal direction, corresponding to σ_1, through an angle ϕ as indicated in Fig. 5.9, then the principal stresses will be σ_1 and $\sigma_2 \cos^2\phi$ and the length of the light path becomes $2t/\cos\phi$; the fringe of order r_ϕ for oblique incidence

$$r_\phi = \frac{2t}{f \cos \phi} (\sigma_1 - \sigma_2 \cos^2 \phi) = \frac{r_1 - r_2 \cos^2 \phi}{\cos \phi}. \qquad (5.22)$$

Solving eqns. (5.21) and (5.22)

$$r_1 = \frac{\cos \phi \; (r_\phi - r \cos \phi)}{\sin^2 \phi}$$

$$r_2 = \frac{r_\phi \cos \phi - r}{\sin^2 \phi}.$$

(5.23)

Substituting eqn. (5.23) into eqn. (5.20) yields the principal stresses σ_1 and σ_2. A similar procedure applies if the model is rotated about the principal direction corresponding to σ_2.

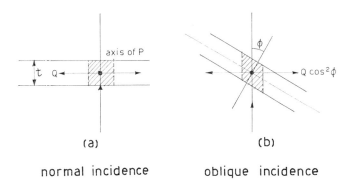

(a)   (b)

normal incidence   oblique incidence

Fig. 5.9.   (a) The model under normally incident light, (b) the model rotated through an angle of ϕ to produce light at oblique incidence.

Let us consider the simple case when in the oblique incidence observations the angle of incidence is 45° (as in Fig. 5.8) and Poisson's ratio for the coating and the model are the same. Then the separate principal stresses are

$$\sigma_1 = \frac{E_m}{t \cdot C_\varepsilon \, (1 + \mu)} \left(\frac{\sqrt{2}}{2} r_{ob} - \tfrac{1}{2} r_n \right)$$

$$\sigma_2 = \frac{E_m}{t \cdot C_\varepsilon \, (1 + \mu)} \left(\frac{\sqrt{2}}{2} r_{ob} - r_n \right).$$

The subscripts *ob* and *n* refer to the retardation in the oblique and normal incidence observations respectively.

The actual relationship between the deformations in a photo-elastic coating and the model to which it is bonded depends on a number of factors: the loading system, temperature variations, strain gradients, differences between Poisson's ratio in the coating and model, and reinforcement effects of the coating. *Reinforcement effects* become acute with thin, flexible models.

In plane stress conditions the fraction of the applied load carried by the coating is directly proportional to the ratio of the thicknesses of the coating and the model, and to the ratio of their elastic moduli; thus, the correction factor

$$\text{C.F.} = 1 + \frac{t_c E_c}{t_m E_m} \cdot \frac{1 + \mu_m}{1 + \mu_c}$$

$$= \frac{(\varepsilon_1 - \varepsilon_2)_{\text{true}}}{(\varepsilon_1 - \varepsilon_2)_{\text{measured}}}$$

where the subscripts c and m refer to the coating and model, respectively. In practice this is often small enough to be ignored. When bending is present, however, two effects must be taken into account. The presence of the coating displaces the neutral axis, and bending produces strain gradients through the thickness of the coating. The observed fringes are proportional to the average strain in the coating, not the strain at the coating/model interface. Fig. 5.10 shows the correction factors for both plane stress and bending as a function of coating to model thickness ratio [5.39, 5.40].

Various plastic sheets and cements are available commercially with C_ε factors varying from 0·04 to 0·16. Using these materials with commercially available reflection polariscopes, it is possible to determine the directions of the principal strains within 2 degrees, and the magnitude of the maximum shear strains to within $\pm$ 10 microstrain.

5.7. Curvature Measurement

When slabs are modelled, the moments in two orthogonal directions M_x and M_y and the twisting moment M_{xy} are required. Moments can be calculated either from surface strains or from radii of curvature. The former method was considered in Section 5.5: measurement of curvature is discussed in this Section.

If there are no membrane forces in the slab and the initial curvature in both directions is zero, eqn. (5.14) becomes:

$$M_x = -\frac{Et^3}{12(1 - \mu^2)}\left(\frac{1}{R_x} + \mu\frac{1}{R_y}\right)$$

$$M_y = -\frac{Et^3}{12(1 - \mu^2)}\left(\frac{1}{R_y} + \mu\frac{1}{R_x}\right)$$

(5.24)

where $R_x = 1/\chi_x$ is the radius of curvature in the x direction and $R_y = 1/\chi_y$ is the radius of curvature in the y direction.

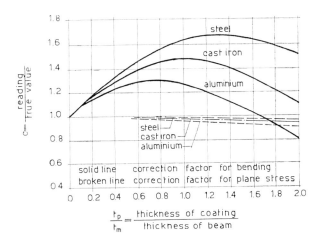

Fig. 5.10. Correction factors for plane stress and bending as a function of coating/model thickness ratio (*from* [4.36]).

The radius of curvature is usually found by measuring the deflection, δ, between two points a distance a apart. Assuming for small deflections a parabolic deflection curve of the slab between these two points, the deflection in the x direction is given by

$$\delta_x = \frac{a^2}{8R_x}$$

and eqn. (5.24) becomes

$$M_x = K(\delta_x + \mu\delta_y)$$

(5.25)

$$M_y = K(\delta_y + \mu\delta_x)$$

where
$$K = \frac{8Et^3}{12a^2(1 - \mu^2)}.$$

To find the magnitude of a bending moment, two curvatures have to be measured, multiplied as in eqn. (5.25) and added together. An instrument has been developed by Leonhardt and Andra [5.41] which does this automatically through an electrical circuit (Fig. 5.11). Its accuracy is excellent since curvature measurements can be made to an accuracy of 1×10^{-7}/mm $\pm 1\%$ ($2\cdot5 \times 10^{-6}$/inch $\pm 1\%$). Since small deflections are sufficient, membrane stresses associated with large deflections can be avoided.

Fig. 5.11. The Curvometer K.E. 2–59 (Krümmungmesser K.E. 2–59) manufactured by Hottinger Messtechnik G.m.b.H.

For each gauge point three moments in the x, y and $45°$ diagonal directions are measured, using eqn. (5.25). The twisting moment

$$M_{xy} = M_{45} - \tfrac{1}{2}(M_x + M_y)$$

and the principal moments, M_1 and M_2, are

$$M_1, M_2 = \tfrac{1}{2}(M_x + M_y) \pm \tfrac{1}{2}\sqrt{(M_x - M_y)^2 + 4M_{xy}^2}.$$

5.8. Loading of Models

The type of loading may affect not only the size, but also the type of model; for example, a model used to determine stresses due to dead loads is generally unsuitable for determining stresses due to earthquakes. The loading on the model is presumed to reproduce faithfully the loads acting on the prototype in terms of magnitude, direction and distribution. Load-approximations are common in model analysis. Uniformly distributed loads are often modelled by a number of point loads. Litle [4.26], investigating the effect of simu-lating distributed loads by concentrated loads in shell buckling problems, found that for domes of 18-inch diameter almost identical results were obtained with uniform pressure, with 61 and with 241 point loads; however, the method of application was significant. Fig. 5.12 shows the difference between point load application through a ball bearing, a washer and a rubber pad.

An approximation in the direction of application of the load is often made, *e.g.* when air bag loading (which produces normal pres-sure) is used to simulate vertical loads on shallow shells. The sequence of application of the loads only becomes important when the response of the structure is non-linear, as in suspension structures.

Various methods of loading are discussed below:

(i) *Dead loading with weights* (*see* Fig. 8.6) is simple and accurate for concentrated loads. It introduces only small errors when used to simulate distributed loads. However, if a large number of points need to be loaded it becomes cumbersome and time consuming to vary the load.

(ii) *Dead loading using the Wiffle tree* (*see* Fig. 8.12) is suitable for static loads. It alleviates the problem of a large number of point loads, since one weight can be used for a large number of points.

(iii) *Hydraulic jacks* (*see* Fig. 8.22) are good for both static and dynamic loading; simultaneous multi-point loading is possible with remote control from a central point. It is useful for cyclic dynamic loading rather than impact loading.

(iv) *Air pressure loading*, usually in the form of air bags, gives a uniform static, normal load to the surface. The bags can be made from laminated polyvinyl chloride sheets, and blown up with a compressor. High loads can be attained. The air bag must be supported by a

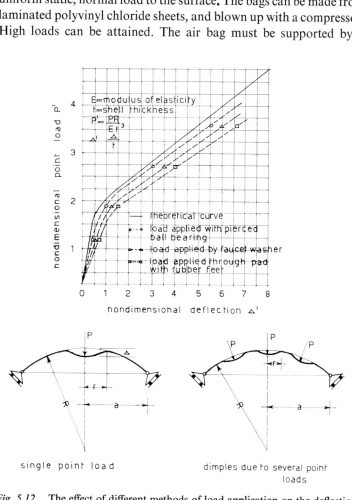

Fig. 5.12. The effect of different methods of load application on the deflections of a dome (*after Litle* [4.26]).

reaction frame. This method is suitable for flat or near-flat surfaces, such as shallow shells.

(v) *Centrifugal force* is used to simulate gravitational loads in structures where self-weight stresses are important.

(vi) *Dynamic forces* are required in the study of stresses produced by earthquakes, impact and vibrations. Suddenly applied loads can be produced by falling weights or pendulums. Mechanical inertia systems and electromagnetic vibration exciters [3.12] are used to produce dynamic loading.

(vii) *Thermal loads* due to temperature variation on one face of the model only (simulating solar radiation) can be produced by placing a heated oil bath on that face. If the thermal action can be considered as due to uniform temperature variation, it suffices to heat the complete model in an oven [3.14].

5.9. *Errors in Experimentation* [5.42]

Model experiments, when used to obtain quantitative results, are subject to a number of sources of error in the physical measurements made. These are:

(i) a failure of the primary sensing element to reflect correctly the measured quantity,

(ii) a failure of the indicating part of the instrument to show correctly the sensing element's response,

(iii) a failure of the observer or recorder to record correctly the instrument reading, and

(iv) a failure of the experimenter to interpret the results correctly.

These errors can be grouped under two headings: systematic errors and random errors. It is important to distinguish between these two, since random errors can be reduced by repeating the experiment a sufficient number of times; systematic errors can neither be directly detected nor compensated for by repetition of the experiment. Fig. 5.13 shows the difference between these two types of errors.

Systematic errors can be caused either by measurement, or by neglect of a variable of secondary importance, or during the inter-pretative process; it is possible, however, to eliminate systematic errors (at least theoretically) once they have been discovered. Random errors can only be minimised. There are a number of methods of checking for systematic error; all these methods assume that random errors have been reduced to a minimum.

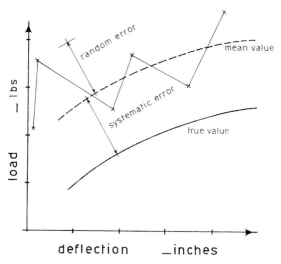

Fig. 5.13. Differentiating between random and systematic errors in the plotting up of an experimental load–deflection curve.

(i) An equilibrium check for loads and reactions, if it can be carried out, is useful for determining the presence of systematic errors. The gross forces on the model are determined either by load cells or by summing the stresses acting on a cross-section; these forces should satisfy equilibrium.

(ii) Symmetric loading of symmetric models should produce symmetric patterns of strains and deflections. If it does not, then systematic errors are present.

(iii) Taking readings during both the loading and unloading stages often shows up systematic errors in the instrumentation.

(iv) It is desirable, but not always possible, to run calibration checks on models. New techniques, in particular, should be first used on simple models where the results are known beforehand to eliminate systematic errors.

Systematic errors due to differing stress–strain curves between model and prototype material occur in most model experiments since it is rare that the same material is used for both. Pahl [4.27] has shown a procedure which determines the bound of this error and helps to minimise it.

Systematic errors due to differing values of Poisson's ratio occur in most model tests, *e.g.* where plastic is used to represent concrete the requirement that the Poisson's ratio for both model and prototype be equal is not satisfied since μ plastic $\approx 0\cdot40$ and μ concrete $\approx 0\cdot16$. The resultant error is systematic in nature. In this case it is better to determine model stresses from model strains, using μ_m, and then convert them to prototype stresses.

An example may illustrate this. Consider an element of a structure in the state of plane strain, *i.e.* all stress and strain components are functions of x and y only and do not vary in a mutually perpendicular, z-direction, therefore all strain components are zero [5.43]. Thus, provided all external influences are in the form of stresses, the stress distribution in the element is independent of Poisson's ratio and the modelling is correct even though $\mu_m \neq \mu_p$. If the model is methyl methacrylate and the prototype is concrete, the material properties are

$E_m = 430{,}000$ lb/sq inch
$E_p = 3{,}000{,}000$ lb/sq inch
$\mu_m = 0\cdot36$
$\mu_p = 0\cdot16$.

If the strains in two perpendicular directions at a point on the model are determined as

$\varepsilon_{xm} = 200 \times 10^{-6}$
$\varepsilon_{ym} = 100 \times 10^{-6}$

the corresponding stress in the x direction in the model can be found using the equation [5.43]

$$\sigma_{xm} = \frac{E_m}{(1 + \mu_m)(1 - 2\mu_m)} [(1 - \mu_m)\,\varepsilon_{xm} + \mu_m\,\varepsilon_{ym}]. \quad (5.26)$$

Substituting the above values into eqn. (5.26) we obtain:

$$\sigma_{xm} = 185 \text{ lb/sq inch.}$$

From the similarity conditions developed in Chapter 3

$$\sigma_p = \frac{E_p}{E_m} \cdot \sigma_m$$

the corresponding stress in the prototype

$$\sigma_{xp} = \frac{3,000,000}{430,000} \times 185 = 1290 \text{ lb/sq inch.}$$

However, if we take $\varepsilon_m = \varepsilon_p$, then $\sigma_{xp} = 455$ lb/sq inch, which is considerably in error.

Random errors can only be treated by probability and statistics [5.44 to 5.48]. Statistics is concerned with two basic problems: descriptive problems and inference problems. The former includes presentation of sets of observations in such a manner that they can be comprehended and interpreted. Inference problems are those involving inductive generalisations, *e.g.* from a sample actually tested to the whole population from which the sample was drawn. Statistical inference enables us to obtain the maximum amount of accurate information from a given effort of testing.

5.10. Planning Structural Model Tests

Structural models are expensive since their construction and testing takes much time and care. Any mistake in either the construction or testing may seriously impair the applicability of the results. Most mistakes occur through insufficient planning of the test, and often a vital reading is omitted. Although there are usually a number of different methods available for determining the unknown quantities, it is important to plan the test to make the best use of the available equipment, time and money.

The main factors can be grouped under eight headings:

(i) *Purpose and extent*: The purpose of the investigation must first be defined. Is it for design or research, laboratory or site investigation? What information is required? Is a complete analysis needed, or will deflections alone suffice? Must the whole field be covered, or is a point-to-point analysis sufficient? Is an elastic analysis adequate, or must behaviour up to failure be studied?

(ii) *Materials*: The choice of the model material is governed by the factors outlined in Section 4.4. Although Perspex (Plexiglas, Lucite), one of the acrylic resins available in sheet form, has been used extensively, it has severe limitations.

(iii) *Measurements required*: These determine to a large extent the instrumentation, depending on whether measurements are to be short-term or long-term, static or dynamic, elastic or inelastic. It is desirable to make a prior assessment of the order of magnitude of the strains, deflections and temperatures to be measured.

(iv) *Instrumentation*: This depends on the measurements required, the environment of the test (whether laboratory or site), the accuracy and the length of time for which the test will run. Availability of equipment, technical assistance, and workshop facilities, are often over-riding factors. Though models may be tested over a period of months, a set of readings is usually completed in one day, so that long term stability of the measuring equipment is rarely important.

(v) *Dimensions and scale*: The approximate size of the model must be decided at the beginning of the investigation; once this has been determined the scale follows. A large model not only takes up more space, but also needs more material, more labour, a larger supporting frame and greater loads. However, less skill and care in the manufacture of a large model produces the same degree of accuracy as a smaller model. A large model also produces larger deflections, and larger strain gauge-lengths may be employed. The optimum model size may be determined by specific cross-sections and lengths, which depend on the similitude relations (*see* Section 3.13). It is always better to use an undistorted model.

(vi) *Loading*: Various methods of applying static, dynamic, gravitational and temperature loads were discussed in detail in Section 5.8.

(vii) *Data analysis*: There is little value in obtaining a large number of readings, if time is not available to reduce and analyse them. This problem can be alleviated by using a digital computer to reduce the data obtained. If statistical analysis is contemplated, it is preferable to establish confidence limits so that the test can be planned accordingly.

(viii) *Cost and time estimation*: In assessing the cost and time required to carry out a model test the principal factors to be considered are:

(a) the cost and time of constructing the model to the required scale and in the appropriate material;
(b) the cost and time of obtaining the measurements necessary to give the desired information reliably;
(c) the cost and time of processing and interpreting the experimental data; and
(d) the time for producing the report.

Stage (a) is likely to take longer than the other three stages combined.

Chapter 6

Visual Models

6.1. The Language of Vision

Like its verbal counterpart, a visual language is a mode of communication. Its effectiveness is measured by its potential to transmit visual information from one participant to another without harmful distortions.

Architecture is a principal determinant of our visual environment and therefore demands the use of effective modes of communication between the architect and his client, consultants and builder. This necessitates a visual language which can be understood by people of diverse backgrounds in visual appreciation. The architect, through his training, acquires a high degree of facility with the two-dimensional representation of three-dimensional concepts. Orthographic drawing is a formalised mode of expression by which forms and shapes are represented in a series of two-dimensional views. It may be considered a highly distorted model representation of the prototype forms and requires some training for its effective application. The perspective drawing seeks to create an illusion of spatial relationships by a geometrical transformation which literally maps the three-dimensional scene onto a plane. Thus, greater visual realism is produced, but at the expense of simplicity: lengths and areas are no longer transformed by constant scale factors, making the perspective unsuitable as a basic form of communication between members of the building team. However, its greater realism is valuable to those less familiar with orthographic drawing.

The main disadvantage of the perspective drawing lies in the use of a fixed observer position which is equivalent to creating the illusion of space without movement. In general, our visual experiences enable an adequate extrapolation to be made from a single perspective drawing. For more complex visual relationships, a number of perspective drawings is often presented making the visual evaluation one of interpretation.

133

Describing reality by projections and perspectives may be likened to the mathematical description (or model) of a physical problem, with similar limitations. Therefore, for complex problems of visual design, the physical model becomes the most effective means of representation. With the model, an observer may study the object from any position and in any desired time sequence. This permits a realistic simulation of the space–time relationship necessary in experiencing architectural forms and spaces. This may be assisted by using a *modelscope*, a miniature periscope, to scale down the observer's field of view. It is also useful for examining the interiors of models (Fig. 6.1), and can be used either as a viewing instrument or as an attachment to a camera for photographic recording. The value of visual model studies may be further extended by the use of motion pictures.

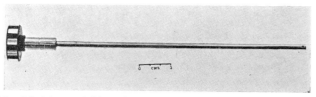

Fig. 6.1. Modelscope. This periscope gives a view of the model, as seen by a person inside the prototype room.

6.2. Visual Design Models

The essential visual elements of architecture are form, space and surface. These are the outcome of an architectural problem conditioned by three performance criteria: aesthetic, technological and economic. The primary purpose of a visual design model is to enable an aesthetic judgement to be made. Technological performance may be assessed by the use of structural and environmental models, whilst economic performance is not readily amenable to physical model simulation.

A suitably designed physical model may yield useful information on both visual and technical factors. This, however, depends on the cost of achieving the requisite model similarity; it may be cheaper to have two models each restricted to its own similarity requirement. Visual models permit considerable distortion, and geometrical similarity alone is generally adequate for modelling form and space. Of the material qualities only texture, transparency and colour are important; but lighting is a significant factor in all visual models.

Models which demonstrate the visual consequences of combinations of form, space and surface are particularly useful to establish perceptual responses. Like the demonstration models of structures, they can be simple and inexpensive, and are often designed to exaggerate in order to achieve greater visual impact.

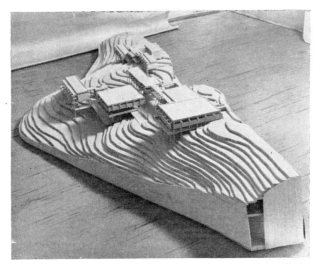

Fig. 6.2.   Visual design model of proposed research centre, made of balsa wood; it was used to relate the structure to the terrain.

While most buildings are initially designed without the aid of visual models, many have architectural models made subsequently to assure the designers and their client that the correct visual evaluation has been made. Since the model is readily understood by the layman, it is useful also for public relations (Fig. 6.2). Paper of various grades, balsa-wood and plywood are most often used in the construction of these models.

When the visual character of the design is complex, such as in free-form shapes, *designing* on the basis of models should be considered. For this type of investigation, a rapid technique of model making permitting easy modification is essential; plasticine, clay, soap and plaster of paris are suitable materials.

6.3. Town Planning Models

The most significant problems of town planning can be portrayed in model form to ensure the design integration of public works (such as bridges, overpasses, and television towers) with the buildings. Physical aspects may sometimes be investigated on the same model, for example, natural lighting, sunshading and airflow around buildings.

6.4. Functional Planning Models

Much time is spent by designers testing alternative functional arrangements on the drawing board, and it is often quicker to employ a three-dimensional scale model.

The functional planning of office and factory interiors, involving the selection of equipment and its disposition, can be carried out with modular co-ordinate components of floors, walls, ceilings and equipment. Interior-layout models are usually suitable for the study of other environmental factors (such as interior lighting in an artificial sky).

Models have recently been used for the co-ordination of the various services within buildings [6.1]. They are constructed from drawings supplied by the consultants, for plumbing, electrical and air-conditioning services, as well as for plant room layout. Aspects of the layout strictly bound by regulations, such as the distance from slab soffits of soil lines, are modelled first, to produce the most logical and economical arrangement, and the other services are then inserted. The building structure is made from transparent plastic so that the services of a number of floors may be seen together. Mistakes made in the design become evident during construction of the model, and this information provides a valuable feedback to the designers. An example of such a model is given in Fig. 6.3 which shows a $\frac{1}{4}$-inch to the foot scale-model of the positions of the services in a forty storey office building recently constructed in Sydney.

This type of model therefore provides not only an X-ray picture of the various three-dimensional services networks, but also a quantitative check on the location of wall and floor penetrations and

Fig. 6.3. Photograph of the services model of the 40-storey N.S.W. Government State Offices Block recently built in Sydney. It was used as an aid to both the designers and the contractor to achieve effective integration of the services with the fabric of the building. (*N.S.W. Public Works Department.*)

other critical factors prior to actual construction. Even after construction the model furnishes a visual record of the services as built, and assists in the training of maintenance personnel.

6.5. Feasibility Study Models

In novel forms of construction it is economical to test the feasibility on a scale model. This enables the designers to assess the performance of their proposed method of construction without erecting a full-scale mock-up.

The roof of the *Sydney Opera House* (Fig. 6.4) was built from precast concrete segments. The main shell arches are made up of a series of ribs, connected to a ridge beam at the apex. The centre line of each rib is located on the great circle of a sphere of radius 246 ft, so that ribs have the same radius but different lengths. Identical cast elements are used for all ribs and located at the same radial distance

Fig. 6.4. The architectural model of the Sydney Opera House showing the ribbed roofing system. (*M. R. Hornibrook Pty. Ltd.*)

from the centre of the great circles. Since two thousand ten-ton segments had to be erected, the contractor designed a *telescopic erection truss* capable of supporting all the ribs without the need for scaffolding.

To test the feasibility of the procedure the contractor built a 1:24 ($\frac{1}{4}$ inch to the foot) brass, fully workable scale model (Fig. 6.5).

The model contained electric motors which caused the truss to elongate the arch arc length whilst maintaining a constant radius, as was required in the prototype. All connections were made through spherical joints onto miniature railway tracks to facilitate longitudinal movement after each rib had been fully erected (Fig. 6.6).

6.6. Demonstration Models

These are designed specifically to demonstrate one or more known aspects of behaviour. Under this heading there is a wide range of models varying both in size and in complexity. *Classroom*

Fig. 6.5(a).   Fig. 6.5(b).

Fig. 6.5. (a) The working model of the telescopic erection truss used to erect the rib segments of the Sydney Opera House. Note the rib partially erected on the far side. (b) the actual telescopic erection truss during the erection of one of the ribs of the prototype. (*M. R. Hornibrook Pty. Ltd.*)

demonstration models are models at their simplest. They should be portable, easy to operate, and simple to comprehend. They can be made from inexpensive materials—even cardboard—and generally demonstrate their point by exaggeration. Because simplicity is required, they have little or no instrumentation. Fig. 6.7 shows a classroom model used to demonstrate the effect of end fixing conditions on deflections in beams, to first year architecture undergraduates.

Laboratory demonstration models are specifically designed for measurement, and thus are accurately made. As they are primarily intended for student use, they should be robust. They may have

Fig. 6.6(a).   Fig. 6.6(b).

Fig. 6.6.   (a) The telescopic section of the model truss. Note also the mechanism for longitudinal movement along the springings of the rib arches, (b) the springing of the erection truss showing the two hydraulic jacks used to move it longitudinally. (*M. R. Hornibrook Pty. Ltd.*)

simple or complex instrumentation, depending on the type of model and the quantities to be measured. Their purpose is to enable students to measure some quantity (such as load, deformation or strain) that has previously been discussed in lectures. Fig. 6.8 shows the test to destruction of a plaster portal frame to determine its ultimate load [6.2, 6.3].

Fig. 6.7. Classroom demonstration model used to demonstrate the effect of end fixing on deflections to undergraduate students. (*Department of Architectural Science, University of Sydney.*)

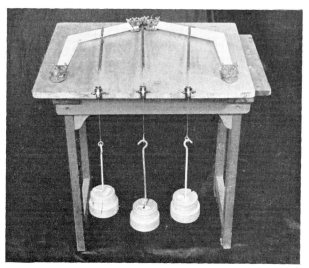

Fig. 6.8. Laboratory demonstration model of a test to destruction of a frame made of plaster of paris, to determine its ultimate load. (*Department of Architectural Science, University of Sydney.*)

Chapter 7

Models and Analogues for Thermal, Acoustical and Lighting Problems

7.1. Functional Efficiency

To be accepted as of good quality, a building requires to be pleasing to the eye, to resist the forces of nature and the ravages of time and to so modify the external environment that it provides pleasant indoor conditions. For this latter, it is generally taken that the thermal, acoustical and lighting conditions should be "correct" and this group of conditions have come to be known collectively as *functional efficiency*. These three by no means exhaust the list of requirements of this type and a full list would also include ventilation, draughts, stuffiness, thermal gradients, echoes, noise, glare and visual appeal.

It will be recognized that one can define the requirement "to resist the forces of nature" as a structural stability and an adequate waterproofness, and "to resist the ravages of time" by the amount of maintenance necessary; these are reasonably definite standards albeit influenced by economic factors. The requirement to be pleasing to the eye inevitably has a measure of fashion included in its assessment. The functional efficiency group is dependent on the subjective assessment of the occupants. These assessments change far less than do fashions in desired appearance, they can probably be related with reasonable precision to physical measurements and unsatisfactory performance can lead to serious and persistent complaints. The standard aimed at, therefore, is precise but not readily defined, it can vary according to the acclimatization of the occupant and it is not necessarily assured by providing conditions that merely agree with the physical measurements aimed at.

7.2. Subjective Standards

The functional efficiency criterion is *comfort*, perhaps more accurately described as lack of discomfort. To ask a group of people if they are thermally uncomfortable or whether they can detect an intruding sound or if a certain light is a glare source is to predispose the majority to say "yes" although they would have continued to accept the intruding effect without complaint if it had not been drawn to their attention. This characteristic of the human sensing mechanism must be well understood in making any experiments or in assessing results to ensure that the correlation with physical measurement is as definite as it appears. Similar care is called for in dealing with "complaints"; the real complaint may be that the conditions objected to are merely different from those experienced in the past, or that a dissatisfaction with one factor has led to a complaint about another.

7.3. Thermal Comfort

Standards of thermal comfort have been established by a "voting" technique. Subjects, after spending some time in a room, are asked to indicate their reaction to the environment. They are asked to assess this in relation to an arbitrary scale:

(i)   very uncomfortably cold
(ii)   uncomfortably cool
(iii) comfortably cool
(iv)   neutral (or comfortable)
(v)   comfortably warm
(vi)   uncomfortably warm
(vii) very uncomfortably hot,

or some pseudonyms of these words; these "votes" are correlated with physical measurements of temperature, humidity, radiation and air movement. From such information, it has been established that preferred temperatures lie somewhere in the range 70°F to 77°F (21°C to 25°C), with part but not all of this variability being caused by differences in clothing. At these temperatures, the effect of humidity appears to be small; the effect of radiation from room walls that average $T°F$ above the air temperature is equivalent to an increase in air temperature of about $T/2°F$ and an air movement of v ft/sec has an effect about equal to a reduction in temperature of $\sqrt{v}/4°F$. An overall change of about 4°F (2°C) will generally lead to a change of "vote" from, say, comfortably cool to neutral and another 4°F to a further change to comfortably warm. Even to achieve the "optimum" temperature will not necessarily ensure that all occupants will agree that comfort conditions have been reached, so great is the person-to-person variability; on the other hand, human tolerance appears to be reasonably large if there is not, say, any air-conditioning equipment and it be understood that "nothing can be done about it".

7.4. Acoustical Comfort

Acoustical comfort is, in some ways, easier to achieve although, in the matter of acoustical privacy, perhaps, even greater problems may arise. The human ear responds to stimuli on a logarithmic scale, *i.e.* successive doubling of the sound energy reaching a listener's ears would be detected as successive small steps of loudness of almost the same size. Two criteria must be fulfilled for acoustical comfort in a room: (i) the sound originating in the room must die away sufficiently slowly that successive echoes from the room surfaces can be integrated by the ear and produce a sound of adequate loudness and yet die away sufficiently rapidly that successive syllables can be separated one from another; and (ii) the unwanted sound or noise originating outside the room must be reduced to a sufficiently low level.

This is not the appropriate place to discuss sound insulation in detail, but a warning should be sounded that in this case also complaints of a particular phenomenon may in fact stem from dissatisfaction with some other feature. It is not only necessary to avoid external sounds being heard in the executive suite, say, but equally important to keep sound (even of shouting?) from within the suite from being understood outside. To know that the noise one makes can be heard outside the particular room or dwelling can reduce one's spontaneity of action.

7.5. Visual Comfort

Visual comfort involves the provision of adequate light intensity, of suitable quality, coming in an acceptable direction and without there being any serious glare sources within the range of vision. Considerable problems can be encountered because occupants are not confined to one position or to looking in a specific direction, there is a great variability of natural light and the common feature of large internal areas with numerous partition walls is to interfere with light transmission. Permanent supplementary artificial lighting is commonly necessary in major buildings, and its provision in a manner suitable both when the natural light is abundant and when it is poor poses severe problems for the lighting engineer.

7.6. Models and Analogues

This chapter is not concerned with the definition of the precise physical environment required by occupants or industrial processes or stored material, but in introducing methods for estimating in advance the probable environment. However, some note should be made of the precision with which the desiderata might be demanded. The architect and his consultants would do well to take care that, in any particular case, the specified tolerances are not reduced far beyond what can be provided at reasonable cost or what is demanded by the occupants, process or storage, for close tolerances can easily lead to greatly increased cost.

Every building or part thereof may be thought of as having an external environment and as modifying that environment by its structure and design to produce the internal environment of the building or room. From the outside to the inside, there will be several transmission paths (for heat, sound or light) from the same or different sources to the inside of the building or room. One may look on internal walls and fittings as sinks to store heat, or absorb sound and light. There may be internal sources of heat, sound or light (that for heat may be for provision or extraction or both) and these may or may not be "controlled" by switches, dampers or thermostats.

A *model* duplicates this network of transmission paths by materials physically similar to the full-size building, at a scale from small- to life-size, and the energy transmitted and property measured as the environment are of the same types as in the full-size building.

An *analogy* duplicates the network with materials dissimilar to those in the building, and the energy transmitted and measured is of a completely different type from that in the building, *e.g.* in an hydraulic analogy for heat flow, the thermal network is represented by a series of tubes, and fluid flow and pressure are used as the "analogies" of heat flow and temperatures.

7.7. Laws of Energy Flow

In a cube of material of infinitesimally small size, the sum of the heat flowing into the six faces must equal the rate of rise of temperature of the cube multiplied by its heat capacity. Given that the law of heat flow is a linear law (this is only roughly true, but the difficult mathematics become impossible if this assumption is not made), which means, in a given case, that doubling the temperature difference doubles the rate of flow of heat, the principle leads to the Fourier equation for heat flow (the diffusion equation):

$$\frac{\partial^2 u}{\partial x^2} + \frac{\partial^2 u}{\partial y^2} + \frac{\partial^2 u}{\partial z^2} = \kappa \frac{\partial u}{\partial t} \qquad (7.1)$$

in which u is the temperature, κ is the thermal diffusivity, $k/C\rho$, where k is the thermal conductivity, C is the specific heat and ρ is the density, and t is the time.

In a building, the bounding surfaces are large in area, and at about the same temperature over the whole of the area at a given depth from the surface, *i.e.* the effect of the corners is small; this means that the flow is largely one-dimensional. For normal buildings, the heat flow through the thickness of the wall is relatively slow (compared, say, to one hour in which time the environment may change noticeably). The total heat flow is proportional to the area of the surface, and is only influenced by the material of the construction and the bounding temperatures and heat flows.

For sound transmission in air (sound velocity is about 1100 ft/sec, audible sounds have frequencies of 20 to 20,000 c/sec and wavelengths varying from 50 ft to $\frac{1}{2}$ inch), the equation derives from the proposition that the excess of the air flow into the unit infinitesimal cube over that flowing out must result in an increase of pressure (the wave equation):

$$\frac{\partial^2 p}{\partial x^2} + \frac{\partial p^2}{\partial y^2} + \frac{\partial^2 p}{\partial z^2} = \frac{1}{c^2}\,\partial^2 p/\partial t^2 \qquad (7.2)$$

where p is the pressure, c is the velocity of sound in air and t is the time. Application of this equation to situations other than "regular" volumes enclosed within acoustically hard walls is seldom possible and generally unrewarding.

For visible light, which is one form of electro-magnetic radiation, the velocity is 186,000 miles/sec, the frequencies extraordinarily high, and wavelengths small. Negligible errors are introduced by the assumptions that the wavelength is extremely small, that scattering at a surface takes place according to the cosine law, and that there is essentially no absorption of the light by the air within the building.

7.8. Thermal Environment

The external thermal environment surrounding a building is modified by the structure to produce the internal environment. The walls are exposed to the external air temperature and subjected to radiation from the sun, sky and surrounding objects; resultant temperatures are modified as heat flows to the inner layers of the wall (as expressed mathematically in the diffusion equation above) and the internal effect is not only dependent on the amount of heat that passes inside but also on the material within the building to be warmed up as the temperature rises. It is easy to see that the resultant external conditions relevant to one wall will differ from those for other walls, for the amount of radiation falling on the various walls is not the same; a further set of resultant conditions will apply to the roof. There are still further heat paths from the outside to inside of a building; heat is transferred by ventilation air, there being an outwards flow of heat if the internal temperature exceeds the external, heat passes through windows by conduction and by transfer of solar radiation. The whole may be thought of as a network connecting various external temperature conditions (being combinations of air temperature and radiation exchange) through thermal paths

such as walls and roofs to the general indoor temperature with, in
turn, the internal heat *sinks* representing the material within the
building which stores heat as the temperature rises. Internally, heat
is exchanged between the bounding surfaces and the air by conduction and convection, and directly between the surfaces by
radiation. As shown by Muncey and Spencer [7.1] it is satisfactorily
accurate to consider both types of transfer by a combined network
connecting each surface to the internal air (as for conduction/
convection alone) although the effective resistance of the surface air
film coefficient should be reduced by 15 to 20 per cent if this be done.

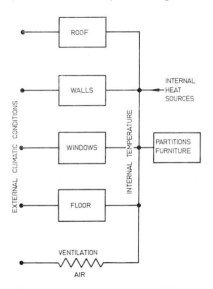

Fig. 7.1. Diagrammatic representation of thermal network.

The whole building may then be considered as a network as
illustrated in Fig. 7.1. The external conditions applicable to the walls
and roof must take account both of the air temperature and the
radiation falling on the surface. This is commonly accounted for by
using the *sol-air* temperature, although the whole concept is still
inadequately supported by quantitative research studies. Any calculation method will need to represent the appropriate network, and
possible techniques using models, analogues and digital calculations

are discussed below. The sol-air temperature for a surface is defined as the equivalent air temperature that would give a heat transfer to or from the surface equal to that caused by the given air temperature and the incident radiation. It is often specified as

$$T_s = T_A + \Sigma(bI)/h \qquad (7.3)$$

where T_s is the sol-air temperature, T_A is the shade air temperature, I is the incident radiation, if necessary separating the various wavelengths, b is the corresponding absorptivity and h is the surface film conductance. It may be measured as the temperature of a surface of the same finish in the same plane backed by a material of zero thermal conductance and zero capacity.

7.9. Stylised Buildings and Thermal Models

Qualitatively it is easy to appreciate that, if the *area* of each and every path of the heat exchange network be changed by a particular factor and if the external conditions remain unchanged, the internal conditions will likewise be unchanged. Provided size is sufficient to keep corner effects small and the ventilation rate is satisfactorily scaled, a model building will have the same internal temperature as its prototype [7.2]. Herein lies the justification for buildings at near full scale representing a particular type, and for the use of scale models at one-quarter and one-ninth scales as reported by Drysdale [7.3]. Figure 7.2 illustrated a colony of thermal models; it will be noted that these are supported well above ground level so that their behaviour will not be derived from the hotter air zone near the ground. Models have the advantage that they may be exposed to an actual climate which greatly reduces the meteorological observations required. Similarly the effect of external colour, orientation and shading may readily be evaluated. Drysdale has published results showing that the temperatures inside the model houses are comparable with those inside the corresponding full-size structures situated nearby, and has made extensive studies of the behaviour of houses based on results from models. Some adjustment of the ventilation rate by trial methods appears to have been necessary in order to obtain temperatures inside the models equal to those in the full-size structure, but how serious this effect would be in further use is not clear from the information available. It may well be that ventilation openings increased from the full size by the scale factor being used would successfully care for this point. Vagaries of the weather can cause a need for very long periods of observation to reach even moderate precision in comparisons; in one test in a Melbourne winter, daily observations over a period of 90 days had to record a difference of $2°F$ ($1°C$) in the average before the difference could be asserted to be statistically significant.

Fig. 7.2. Thermal models of domestic and industrial type buildings. (*Commonwealth Experimental Building Station, Australia*).

7.10. Thermal Analogues

If one were able to find other physical phenomena that could be described by the diffusion equation, eqn. (7.1), then an analogue of suitable network form and component values could be used for internal temperature calculations. It is desirable that in the analogue network the inherent time constants involved be considerably smaller than in a building and be variable at the designer's wish, and further, that the network be one in which the physical measurements are simpler than in the thermal network. Electrical and hydraulic analogues [7.4, 7.5 and 7.6] satisfy these requirements.

One further change is desirable to facilitate the construction of these analogues. Thermal resistance and capacity are distributed uniformly through a homogeneous slab of material, but this configuration is not readily duplicated in electrical and hydraulic components. In practice, therefore, lumped values of resistance and capacity are used, normally in arrangements consisting of a sequence of T- or π-sections (usually equal sections) and arranged so that the total resistance and total capacity are the same as would occur in the "precise" analogy. It has been shown that reasonable precision (1 to 2 per cent) is achieved in most cases if any homogeneous slab is represented by three sections. An electrical analogy has been constructed by Danter [7.7].

In the thermal network, the units for a wall thickness of 1 inch might be:

$$\text{resistance } °F \text{ ft}^2 \text{ h/Btu}$$

$$\text{capacity Btu/}°F \text{ ft}^2$$

and the unit of resistance by capacity, *i.e.* time, is one hour. If the choice in electrical units be, say, 10,000 ohms and 1 micro F respectively, the period in the analogy corresponding to 1 hour in the thermal case will be 0·01 sec. It is possible to vary the choice of electrical units, although obviously the choice of any two of the resistance, capacity and time scales fixes the third. There remains a further choice of electrical e.m.f. (voltage) or current to represent temperature or heat flow, and selection of one value (given the resistance scale is fixed) predetermines the other.

Analogues are particularly convenient for estimating the likely internal conditions in a building and the effect that a modification of the design will introduce. Like any calculating device, be it analogue or digital, the precision of the answers depends on the accuracy of the representation of physical laws and of the external or boundary conditions introduced. Thermal conductivity and capacity are both assumed constant in this and other calculation methods (and in eqn. (7.1)), estimates of external air temperature take no account of its variation with height, the effect of change in external film resistance with wind and height is not considered, and how to introduce the effect of radiation is not precisely known. In the main, neglecting these short-comings does not appear to introduce serious errors.

The particular advantage of the electrical analogy is the possibility of modifying the network during the cycle, *e.g.* one may increase the "ventilation rate" during hot periods when the internal temperature exceeds the external or duplicate the behaviour of a thermostat or other control. Special rather than general-purpose equipment is normally used for thermal analogies, and recent examples commonly use periods of a fraction of a second to represent one hour in the thermal case; electronic techniques are adopted for driving voltages, measuring equipment and necessary non-linear devices.

7.11. Electronic Digital Calculation

As an alternative to calculation with an analogue, the digital evaluation of internal temperature may be adopted. The network is of similar form to those described earlier and, in one method, a lumped network is considered and its thermal configuration calculated on a step by step basis. In each individual capacity–resistance group, the temperature difference between the capacities divided by the connecting resistance and multiplied by time is an estimate of the heat flow during the period, and the resultant change in temperature of the capacities can be evaluated and applied. Proceeding through the network in this way and repeating for successive times enables the internal temperature and any heat flows of interest to be evaluated. Change in the configuration of the network, changes in resistance or capacity values, and representations of the effect of thermostats and controls can all be introduced; the initial temperature distribution assumed has no effect on results if an adequate time is allowed for its effects to fall to zero [7.8].

If the network remains unchanged and if external conditions repeat, a method often referred to as the matrix method may be used. It depends on the fact that, if temperatures and heat flows are everywhere cyclical and sinusoidal, the various heat paths may be considered as passive four-poles and the network "solved" [7.9, 7.10, 7.11]. If the cycle be non-sinusoidal, it is obviously possible to resolve it into a series of harmonics, to solve the network at each frequency and to find the internal temperature by subsequent Fourier synthesis. The arithmetical work in either method is tedious, but appropriate for an electronic digital computer.

The advantages and disadvantages of the method parallel those of the analogue method. Specialized equipment is not required; with the matrix method no change in the basic network during the cycle is possible with present knowledge, although attempts are being made to overcome this.

7.12. Acoustical Environment

The sound field within a room will obviously be the summation of a part from the sound generated within the room and a part transmitted from outside. In small rooms—to, say, 5000 cu ft volume—the prime factor related to the sound generated within the room is the provision of a reasonable amount of acoustical absorbent material. Without it the room will be far too *live*, a factor which is commonly qualified by the reverberation time, defined as the time required for the sound level within a room to decrease by 60 dB (energy ratio $10^6:1$) after the cessation of the sound source. Values of the order of 0·5 to 1·2 sec are desirable and may be estimated from the Sabine formula:

$$T = \frac{V}{20 \, \Sigma \, AS} \tag{7.4}$$

where T is the reverberation time in seconds, V is the volume of the room in cu ft and $\Sigma \, AS$ is the absorption contribution of each area S sq ft multiplied by its absorption coefficient A.

For larger rooms, halls and auditoria, the internal sound field normally demands considerably more attention, particularly because such buildings can often only fulfil their purpose if the acoustics be good. They are commonly of such cost that considerable design effort is warranted and the various model and analogy methods considered below are applicable for such cases.

Sound from external sources will penetrate into the room through any openings and by transmission through the bounding structure. Energy reductions of sound level from outside to inside commonly require to be in the range 10^3 to 10^5 to 1 (30 to 50 dB), and this often demands heavy structures (5–50 lb/sq ft of wall area), or considerable distance between the source of the intruding noise and the room of interest.

7.13. *Acoustical Analogues for Auditoria*

The basic criteria for provision of good acoustics in rooms are satisfactory reverberation time, adequate echoes from walls or ceiling shortly following the sound received directly from the source, and reasonable diffusion or lack of echo concentration [7.12]. The adjustment of the reverberation time is commonly controlled by estimates based on the Sabine equation, eqn. (7.4) or other refined but comparable formula. Some care is desirable to ensure that the absorption is not largely in areas where little sound impinges.

Sound from most sources is nearly omnidirectional and studies are often undertaken to follow the paths of the sound. One obvious method, considerably simpler in two dimensions than in three, is by a drawing board technique. This analogy uses lines to represent the path of the sound rays. The paths commence at the point corresponding to the sound source, and whenever they meet a bounding surface the assumption is made of specular reflection with equal angles of incidence and reflection. Rays are followed through a considerable number of reflections with the assumption that the ray energy is inversely proportional to the distance travelled squared, and that its time of arrival is delayed by an amount proportional to the distance travelled. Such analogy studies can become most complex, and this difficulty obviously increases greatly if attempts are made to perform it on a three-dimensional basis. The use of this method in part of the basis for rating the acoustical excellence of halls is discussed by Beranek [7.13].

Some reduction in experimental and drawing complexity can be achieved by using a light ray as an analogy for the sound ray and providing surfaces at appropriate positions which will suitably reflect the light. In this method, a light source is placed in a position analogous to that of the sound source, and the light intensity distribution is explored to detect variations in the distribution pattern, echo concentrations and *dead* spots [6.2]. It can be seen that the analogue surfaces can be made absorbing to the light waves approximately as for sound and, if desired, non-specular in character. It is not possible by this method to make studies of the time of delay in propagation along the various paths because of the great speed of light, but apart from the need to ensure some echoes with short delays (which can be studied by the drawing technique) this is not a serious disadvantage. Such analogues have been constructed to study aspects of hall design, but, so far as is known, no hall design has been completely based on such techniques.

7.14. Acoustical Models for Auditoria

Examination of the equation for the propagation of sound will show that, if the space dimensions and the time are changed in the same ratio, the equation is satisfied by the same pattern in the solution. This implies that if a model at a scale $1/n$ of the full size be constructed, and if the time be changed in the same ratio (*i.e.* the sound frequency is increased in the ratio $n/1$), the sound field in the model will be similar to that in the full size. It will be realized that the model surfaces must duplicate the surfaces in the full size, and that the acoustical properties of the surfaces at the relevant frequencies (in the proportion $n/1$) are the same. This is not easy to achieve for other than acoustically-hard surfaces, but is obviously essential, for one knows subjectively the change that acoustical absorbents can make to the acoustics of a space with hard walls and considerable reverberation. It is often contended that the increased absorption of sound by air as the frequency increases invalidates this model hypothesis. The law required for a precise model is that the absorption per unit distance of propagation be proportional to the frequency. Classical theories suggest the absorption appears to be more nearly proportional to frequency squared; but on experimental data the absorption appears to be more nearly proportional to the frequency. This aspect would need careful attention before any complete reliance were placed on acoustical assessments based on model tests.

Such models (Figs. 7.3 and 7.4) have been shown to provide a means of estimating the behaviour of a full-size hall [7.14, 7.15] with a precision equal to that to be expected from the precision of the matching of the surface properties. Matching of the model surfaces is not easy. The necessary property to be matched is the specific acoustic impedance; it is not easy to measure with precision, especially for absorbent materials, and the matching of model surfaces over an adequate frequency range requires a large number of trials to discover a suitable surface. Further it is insufficient merely to ensure a

Fig. 7.3. Acoustical model at one-quarter scale of a large room. (*Division of Building Research, CSIRO, Australia.*)

Fig. 7.4. Acoustical model at one-tenth scale of a public hall. (*Division of Building Research, CSIRO, Australia.*)

good matching of surface absorption, for an associated requirement is an equal precision in model dimensions (to, say, 1/20 of a wavelength) which may prove difficult to achieve.

The usage of such models does not appear to be promising, however, for the synthesis by the human ear and mind of the complex sounds heard does not match the complexity that can be established by instrumental measurements. For instance, if two identical sequences of sound reach the listener from sources so arranged that one sequence is delayed by, say, 30 msec (0·03 sec) behind the other and both are of equal loudness, the listener will be conscious of only one source (the first) and will assess the loudness as 3 dB (*i.e.* twice the energy) greater than the first source. It seems extremely unlikely that any increased precision in our measurements of auditoria acoustics will ever be necessary, because the ultimate listening device is the combination of two human ears and the human brain, and the sensing ability of this combination is unlikely to change. For speech, the requirement is that one may understand the message of the speaker, and because of the considerable redundancies in normal speech communication this can be achieved even if all syllables are not heard perfectly. The human mind is able to make corrections, or selections of alternatives of possible sounds, so that the whole sentence or speech fits logically together. With music, likewise, the performer does not seek to bring precise information to the listener, but rather to interpret the composition so that the mood, the inspiration and the message of the work may influence and inspire his listeners. Again some lack of precision in transmission does not seriously hamper this purpose.

Suggestions are frequently made that this technique of acoustical models could be extended to "listen" to the acoustics of a projected hall. Music recorded in an environment where no echoes were generated (difficult for musical performers who find ensemble hard to achieve in such circumstances) would be replayed at increased speed—ratio $n/1$—in the model and the sound at a selected position recorded. Replaying at slower speed—ratio $1/n$—would then, it is claimed, give a "preview" of the acoustics of a projected auditorium. For this to be achieved, it would be necessary:

 (i) to have a model whose surfaces provided an adequate

representation of the full-size structure over a range of seven octaves, say (100 to 12,800 c/s);

(ii) to have tape or other recorders which did not introduce excessive distortion over this frequency range in a number of record/ replay cycles;

(iii) to have a recorder and transducer devices capable of working accurately at the increased frequencies.

Since certainly the first and third, and, to a lesser extent, the second of these cannot at present be realized, suggestions for the use of some such method, whilst theoretically possible, are not likely to become practical for a considerable time.

7.15. Acoustical Models and Analogues for Transmission

Transmission of sound from one room of a building to another may take place through the intervening wall or floor–ceiling combination. The sound in the source room forces the bounding surfaces to vibrate at the sound frequencies and these in turn act as a sound source in the neighbouring room. The effective insulation is largely dependent on the superficial weight (lb/sq ft) of the wall or floor. A wall of 5 lb/sq ft gives a sound transmission loss of about 30 dB (10^3:1) and this increases about 5 dB for every time the weight is doubled. The sound may also be transmitted via ducts and openings between rooms, and clearly no model or analogue is necessary or useful in assessing the sound transmitted between rooms by either of these processes.

Some sound also passes to the receiving room by *flanking* transmission—side wall vibrations induce movements in both the intervening wall between the rooms and the side walls of the receiving room. The laws governing such transfer of energy are not well known and the transfer generally is small (10^5:1), so it is unlikely that calculations of its magnitude whether by use of models, analogues or digital calculation will be needed often and no such calculations have been reported.

Transmission of sound in the open air past obstacles is a situation where calculations may well be required, and where models would be particularly suitable. One of the best and most frequently neglected methods of reducing noise levels at critical places, is to separate the sound source and the listener and to introduce barriers between. A model, generally using acoustically hard surfaces and employing sound at increased frequency, would represent the actual conditions with good precision, and the use of such models for studying the noise transmission characteristics of building layouts would be most useful. Some specialized transducer equipment may be needed for such models, but otherwise readily available techniques could be employed.

7.16. Visual Environment

The visual environment requires that there must be adequate light of acceptable quality coming from a suitable direction, and without any accompanying glare sources. This general specification needs to be related to the particular case. Provision of light may be achieved by natural or artificial light or a combination of both, and naturally the required specification must be met at all times and by the particular combination of light sources.

7.17. Visual Models

Because of the facts that light transmission takes place essentially instantaneously, that the absorption of light by surfaces can be easily duplicated, that the wavelength is so small that accurate scaling of the wavelength is irrelevant and that measurements can be made with adequate precision, light models are relatively easy to construct and use; there is no need to seek analogous phenomena as a basis for analogue calculations.

Models of whole buildings and of groups of buildings may be exposed to model daylight and measurements made. The daylight may represent sunlight and the model method used to assess sunlight and shaded surfaces; a spotlight is used for such purposes, and light and model may be moved relatively to one another to examine the situation at various times of the day and dates of the year. Such equipment is illustrated in Fig. 7.5.

The behaviour of buildings and rooms under natural light from a dullish overcast sky is studied using an artificial sky. Some discussion still takes place as to how to place the electric lamps to achieve the "correct" distribution, but the principle is to have a hemi-spherical surface lighted from around and below the edges of a circular plane which represents the earth. Models of a building, or even a sequence of buildings to represent a city street (*see* Fig. 7.6), can be placed under an artificial sky and the behaviour studied.

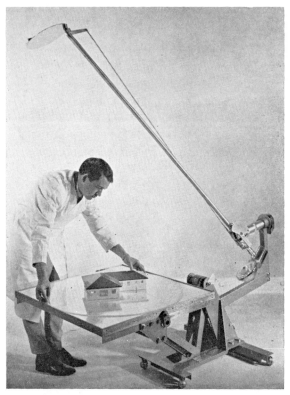

Fig. 7.5. The solarscope; a device for studying, with models, shadows to be cast by buildings. (*Commonwealth Experimental Building Station, Australia.*)

Models of rooms lit by artificial light are often constructed at full size so that different arrangements may be studied or demon-strated. In such cases, the aspects of models and analogies being discussed here are relatively insignificant, and the method of making the model of lighting and testing it is obvious and straightforward.

Models of artificial illumination have been used also for measurement and demonstration in such instances as the lighting of streets and of pedestrian crossings for motorways (Fig. 7.7). By such means, and at a fraction of the cost of full-scale installation, it is possible to explore alternate means of achieving a desired end, and of demonstrating in advance the likely efficacy of any method proposed.

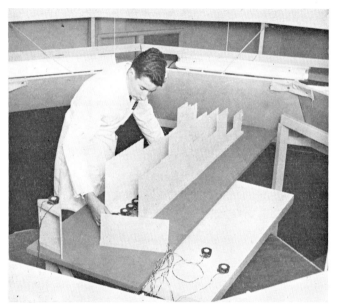

Fig. 7.6.   Study of the availability of daylight in streets bounded by tall buildings
(*Commonwealth Experimental Building Station, Australia.*)

7.18. *The Advantages of Models and Analogues*

A building is likely to be satisfactory only if its functional efficiency can be described as adequate. Reasonable correlation had been found between the subjectively desirable criteria and certain physical measurements. Models and analogies can be used to calculate the likely internal environment, and predictions may be made whether this will be satisfactory or whether design changes are required.

Models and analogies facilitate this work and enable it to be pursued at comparatively less cost than full-scale work. Investiga-

Fig. 7.7(a)

Fig. 7.7(b)

Figs. 7.7(a) *and 7.7*(b).   Demonstration by use of models of lighting at a pedestrian crossing. (*Division of Physics, CSIRO, Australia.*)

tions may be extended to study the principles involved, and the reduced cost permits greater replication for a given total expenditure. Models suffer from the deficiencies inherent in modelling at small scale the properties of the full-size structure, and suffer in accuracy if the physical laws in the smaller size do not give exactly the same effect as in the full-size building. Analogies and digital calculation demand an even more precise knowledge of the physical laws, and of the external conditions to be encountered. In a specific case the choice of method may be marginal, but the result, being far better than that available by sophisticated estimates, is likely to lead to improved internal environmental conditions.

Chapter 8

Some Applications of Models to Architectural Problems

8.1. Introduction

Previous chapters outlined the main areas of application and the available methods of model studies in architecture and related fields. This chapter is devoted to the presentation and discussion of various applications of model analysis to actual problems. It is hoped that these case histories will illustrate the practical applications of model methods.

Generally, the construction and instrumentation of models is more difficult than the interpretation of the results. For this reason the construction and instrumentation of the models is fully described, whereas the interpretation is discussed in detail only for difficult cases, such as distorted models.

8.2. Model of Continuous Shell Roof for C.I.B.A.*

This is a reinforced concrete roof consisting of twelve cylindrical south-light shells arranged to form a four-bay, three-span continuous roof complex. The shell is 3 inches thick, rising 9 ft in section, and has a 24 ft radius of curvature. Both top and bottom edge beams are provided, and four tubular steel window posts connect the upper edge of one shell to the bottom edge of the adjacent one.

This shell roof was the first of its kind built in Australia. Being unsymmetrical as well as continuous, the structural design of the shell presented, at that time, considerable analytical difficulties, and could only have been solved on the basis of using either very approximate boundary conditions in an exact solution, or an approximate solution with the correct boundary conditions. In addition some

---

* *Consulting Engineers*: Miller, Milston, Ferris. *Architect*: Harry Seidler.

unexpectedly large deflections were observed on the first three shells completed. Consequently a programme of model analysis and field measurements was initiated by the consulting engineers in association with the Department of Architectural Science, University of Sydney.

The purpose of the model analysis was to confirm the approximate elastic analysis, and to provide data for correlation with the field measurements. Ignoring temperature and dynamic effects, the significant similarity conditions are obtainable from Table 8.1,

Table 8.1
Similarity conditions for continuous shell model

Parameters	Prototype	Model	Scale Factors	Comments
Length	l_p	l_m	λ_l (48)	By choice
Elastic modulus	E_p (4×10^6 lb/sq in)	E_m (5×10^5 lb/sq in)	λ_E (8)	By choice
Poisson's ratio	μ_p (0·2)	μ_m (0·35)	$\lambda_\mu = 1$ (0·6)	Not fulfilled
Force	P_p	P_m	$\lambda_p = \lambda_E \lambda_l^2$ (18,500)	Easily fulfilled
Strain	ε_p	ε_m	$\lambda_\varepsilon = 1$	Easily interpreted
Stress	σ_p	σ_m	$\lambda_\sigma = \lambda_E$ (8)	Easily interpreted
Displacement	u_p	u_m	$\lambda_u = \lambda_l$	Similarity of deformation

Note: subscripts p and m denote prototype and model respectively, λ_l denotes scale factor for parameter l, etc.

which lists the significant parameters together with the scale factors used. As two basic dimensions, force and length, are sufficient for a complete dimensional analysis, two of the resulting scale factors can be arbitrarily chosen, and it was convenient to fix these for length and elastic modulus, *i.e.* λ_l and λ_E. To model the important continuity effects, six shell units were considered necessary. Modelling the 3-inch concrete membrane by $\frac{1}{16}$-inch Perspex fixed the length scale factor at 48; the resulting model had overall dimensions approximately 40 inches by 11 inches, a size suitable for laboratory study. Instantaneous values of Young's modulus for the concrete and Perspex were assumed to be 4×10^6 and 5×10^5 lb/sq inch, respectively, while Poisson's ratios were taken as 0·2 and 0·35, respectively. Numerical values of elastic constants and scale factors are shown in Table 8.1 inside the brackets. Some error was incurred by the Poisson's ratio distortion; but this was considered secondary for reinforced concrete structures of this type. An additional minor error arising from modelling the tubular steel window posts by solid Perspex was also ignored.

The shell membranes were all taken from the same sheet of plastic and were readily formed around a heavy gauge steel mould after the required softening in a temperature-controlled oven. The shell, lying between the mould and sand-bags, was then allowed to cool slowly in the oven to minimize differential temperature distortion. Edge beams and columns were cut from sheets of plastic of appropriate thickness, and glued to the shells to produce a model with a high degree of continuity. The completed model was mounted on a sturdy steel frame. Movable cross bars supported the deflection gauges (Fig. 8.1).

Fig. 8.1. Plastic model of two bays of the C.I.B.A. shell during testing. Strain readings are being taken by both Huggenberger tensometers and electrical resistance strain gauges; deflection readings are taken with dial gauges.

The model was loaded by three separate systems of suspended weights: top edge beam, bottom edge beam and shell membrane. Preliminary tests established that a load 2·4 times the scaled load yielded measurable strains without excessive deflections or non-linear effects. This factor is included in the interpretation of the strain and deflection readings. Instrumentation consisted of electrical resistance strain gauges (Philips PR 9214 120 ohm gauges with 4 mm gauge length) for the shell membrane, Huggenberger tensometers for the edge beams and Baty dial gauges (reading to 0·001 inch) for deflections. Two portable strain gauge bridges were employed with dummy electrical resistance gauges mounted on Perspex placed immediately adjacent to the model. It was considered important to study the effect of loading the edge beam and shell membrane separately and, accordingly, the loading cycle consisted of load bottom beam—load shell—load top beam—unload top beam—unload shell—unload bottom beam. As the shell strains were very small, the electrical resistance strain gauges were connected directly to the measuring bridge to minimize contact resistance variations. About 15 minutes were allowed for each gauge to reach thermal equilibrium; thereafter the effects of creep in the plastic were minimized by taking instantaneous readings after each loading operation. This procedure justified the use of instantaneous values for the Young's modulus. Long-term effects on the prototype could be estimated by the use of an effective modulus.

8.3. Model of Steel Frame, Chevron-Hilton Hotel, Sydney*

The proposed Stage II of the Sydney Chevron-Hilton Hotel is unusually tall and narrow (height/width ratio approximately 9), so that deflection due to wind and the stresses caused by wind loading are of particular importance. This is accentuated because the proposed 40-storey building for stage II is placed at right-angles to the existing 14-storey stage I building (Fig. 8.2) such that the differential deflection of the two buildings over the lower fourteen storeys is of special interest.

---

* *Consulting Engineers*: Wargon, Chapman and Associates. *Architect*: Donald E. Crone.

The model test (Fig. 8.3) was undertaken by the Department of Architectural Science, University of Sydney, at the request of the consulting engineers, to provide preliminary data on the deflection of the unclad steel frame and the stresses at the joints of the beams and columns under horizontal loading. This project was the first high-rise building proposed for Sydney; computer programs for the structural analysis of multi-storey buildings of this size were unavailable, so that a model investigation was required.

Fig. 8.2. Photograph of visual model of both stage I and stage II of the Chevron-Hilton Hotel, Sydney.

In a small-scale model of a steel structure it is impossible to reproduce the exact shape of the steel sections and some distortion of geometric similarity must be accepted. The deflection y_1 of a linearly elastic structure at any point *1* due to a force P_2 applied at any point *2* can be expressed as

$$y_1 = P_2 \left(K_a \cdot \frac{l}{EA} + K_b \cdot \frac{l^3}{EI} + K_s \cdot \frac{l}{GA} + K_t \cdot \frac{l^3}{GJ} \right) \quad (8.1)$$

where l is the length of member, A is the cross-sectional area, I is the second moment of area, J is the polar second moment of area, E is the elastic modulus, G is the modulus of rigidity and K_a, K_b, K_s and K_t are constants accounting for relative effects of axial force, bending moment, shear force and torsional moment.

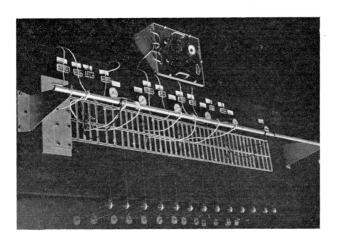

Fig. 8.3. The plastic structural model of one frame of stage II of the Chevron-Hilton Hotel under test. Lateral deflection readings were taken at the 6th, 11th, 18th, 25th, 32nd and 40th floors with dial gauges.

If the four actions are simultaneously significant, complete geometrical similarity (and the equality of Poisson's ratio) must be observed between the prototype and the model. However, for a tall building bending predominates, so that eqn. (8.1) becomes

$$y_1 = P_2\left(K_b \cdot \frac{l^3}{EI}\right) \qquad (8.2)$$

Using eqn. (8.2) to obtain the expression relating prototype deflections to model deflections we get:

$$\frac{y_p}{y_m} = \frac{P_p}{P_m} \cdot \frac{K_b \cdot l_p^{\,3}}{E_p \cdot I_p} \cdot \frac{E_m \cdot I_m}{K_b l_m^{\,3}} \qquad (8.3)$$

but

$$\frac{y_p}{y_m} = \frac{l_p}{l_m} = \lambda_l$$

$$\frac{E_p}{E_m} = \lambda_E$$

and

$$\frac{I_p}{I_m} = \lambda_I$$

and so

$$\frac{P_p}{P_m} = \frac{\lambda_E \lambda_I}{\lambda^2_l} = \lambda_p. \qquad (8.4)$$

Eqn. (8.4) indicates that the scale factor for the second moment of area may assume values not related to λ_l. It justifies making a detail length scale factor λ_r different from the overall length scale factor λ_l.

For the model, a layout scale factor of 100 was chosen which reduced the 450-ft-high frame to a manageable model length of 53·4 inches. The model sections were designed to keep the proportion between the second moment of area of the prototype and model sections constant. This avoided the labour and expense of machining to reproduce the prototype built-up beam section. This changes three times in each of the lower beams, and in one bay the section is further modified by holes in the web to allow passage of service ducts. Perspex sheet $\frac{1}{4}$ inch thick was used throughout, as this gave a ratio of width to depth in the model corresponding to the largest number of prototype members. In the prototype the second moment of area is varied by adding steel plates to the basic steel section; this alters the overall depth of the section only slightly. In the model, the change in the second moment of area was achieved by altering the depth of the section cut from the uniformly thick Perspex sheet. Thus, all model beams and columns had a uniform width of $\frac{1}{4}$ inch, while the depth varied appreciably.

Consequently, it was only possible to maintain the correct scale ratio for the distance between the centres of the members, or for the clear distance between them. To minimise the error introduced by this effect, the scale factor for the cross-sectional dimensions was reduced to 70. This gives correct scaling at the 14th floor, which is the top of the stage I building. At all other floors the distance between the centres of members was scaled correctly, but the effective length of the model columns was slightly too high at the upper floors and too low at the bottom floors.

The model was cut from a single sheet of Perspex with a fret-saw and finished by filing with progressively finer files. At this stage it was possible to make an accurate correction for the variation in thickness of commercially available Perspex sheet: each member was checked for width before filing, and the depth then adjusted in accordance with the requirement of the correct second moment of area for that member. The service ducts were simulated by drilled holes $\frac{1}{16}$ inch in diameter, and the web-cleats by necking the section with a triangular file to half depth.

The model was tested horizontally, resting on stainless steel rollers to minimise friction. The loads were applied horizontally at panel points (Fig. 8.3). Deflection measurements were made with dial gauges placed on the windward side of the model: the effect of the spring-loaded gauges was treated as an initial loading. Strain measurements were taken at the top and bottom of each beam and column converging on certain floor junctions. Since the model was tested for horizontal load only, direct stresses were assumed as negligible by comparison with bending stresses. The electrical resistance strain gauges at the top and bottom of the beam sections were therefore connected in pairs to form a half-bridge, thus making dummy gauges unnecessary, as well as doubling the gauge sensitivity. The gauges were waterproofed.

The *interpretation* of the model measurements is made complex by the distortion in model sections, *i.e.* $\lambda_l = 100$ and $\lambda_r = 70$ (exact at the 14th floor). Consider the ratio of prototype and model moments:

$$\frac{M_p}{M_m} = \frac{P_p l_p}{P_m l_m}$$

$$= \lambda_p \lambda_l. \tag{8.5}$$

Substitute for λ_p from eqn. (8.4) to get:

$$\frac{M_p}{M_m} = \frac{\lambda_E \lambda_I}{\lambda_l}. \tag{8.6}$$

The ratio of the prototype and model stresses is given by:

$$\frac{\sigma_p}{\sigma_m} = \frac{M_p Z_m}{M_m Z_p} \qquad (8.7)$$

where $Z = I/\frac{1}{2}d$ (section modulus), so eqn. (8.7) becomes:

$$\frac{\sigma_p}{\sigma_m} = \frac{M_p}{M_m} \cdot \frac{I_m}{d_m} \cdot \frac{d_p}{I_p}.$$

Substituting for M_p/M_m from eqn. (8.6) and λ_I for I_p/I_m to get:

$$\frac{\sigma_p}{\sigma_m} = \frac{\lambda_E}{\lambda_I} \cdot \frac{d_p}{d_m}. \qquad (8.8)$$

The substitution $d_p/d_m = \lambda_r$ is not admissible in this equation because the model is designed to reproduce I but not d. From eqn. (8.8) the relation between strains in the prototype and the model is:

$$\frac{\varepsilon_p}{\varepsilon_m} = \frac{\sigma_p}{\sigma_m} \cdot \frac{E_m}{E_p},$$

substituting for σ_p/σ_m from eqn. (8.8) to get:

$$\frac{\varepsilon_p}{\varepsilon_m} = \frac{1}{\lambda_I} \cdot \frac{d_p}{d_m} \qquad (8.9)$$

Eqn. (8.9) gives the direct transformation of model strain into prototype strain, the ratio d_p/d_m being known from previous calculation.

The model showed satisfactory behaviour and was found to remain elastic without buckling at 5 times the model working load. It was tested for three conditions of loading:

(i) a uniformly distributed horizontal load of 600 lb per vertical foot run;

(ii) a uniformly distributed horizontal load of 600 lb per vertical foot run, plus a superimposed load of 250 lb per vertical foot run above the 28th floor;

(iii) a concentrated horizontal force of 100,000 lb at the 35th floor to give an estimate of the effect of accidental loading, say, due to an aircraft crashing into the building.

The resulting deflection profiles are shown in Fig. 8.4. The deflections of the completed building would be much less than those of the unclad frame because of the composite action of the cladding, floors and masonry walls with the frame.

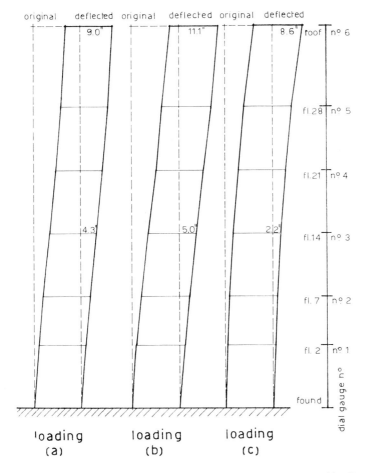

Fig. 8.4. The deflected shape of the unclad steel frame under three lateral loading conditions. (a) A uniformly distributed lateral load of 600 lb per vertical foot run, (b) loading as in (a) plus a superimposed load of 250 lb per vertical foot run, above the 28th floor, (c) a concentrated lateral load of 100,000 lb at the 35th floor.

8.4. *Model Analysis of Plated Dome Roof* *

The domed, folded-plate roof of the Granville Returned Service League's Club, Sydney, provides an example of a structure which is well suited to direct model analysis. The design is based on three intersecting circles, the outer circles being roofed by reinforced concrete folded plates in the form of a dome. The larger dome has a diameter of 86 ft (29 m) and is formed by three annular plates intersected by three conical rings. This unusual structure has no simple analytical solution and additional complications are introduced by the irregular support conditions.

A model test (Fig. 8.5) was undertaken by the Department of Architectural Science, University of Sydney, at the request of the consulting engineers to provide data on the deflection of the dome

Fig. 8.5. Plastic structural model of plated dome roof showing positioning of dial gauges for deflection reading and method of loading. The scale of the model is 1 : 32.

---

* *Consulting Engineers*: Miller, Milston, Ferris. *Architect*: Frank Fox and Associates.

and on the stresses at certain points under a uniformly distributed vertical load. In particular, information was required on the maximum deflection and on the stress distribution along one of the radii.

Although the dome is of complex shape, the component parts are mostly flat, and the model was therefore machined from sheets of Perspex and welded together. Comparable dimensional accuracy could not have been achieved with a casting resin without significant increase in both time and cost.

The modulus of elasticity of Perspex was obtained from a flexure test on a bar cut from one of the sheets. Average results obtained are given in Table 8.2. Particular importance was attached to the deflection measurements and care was taken to allow the gauges to settle; the modulus of elasticity was taken as 400,000 lb/sq inch. The instantaneous modulus of elasticity of concrete was taken as 4×10^6 lb/sq inch, giving a modular ratio, $\lambda_E = 10$. For assessing the deflections after a specified period of time an effective modulus of 2×10^6 lb/sq inch was assumed to allow for short-term creep; the corresponding modular ratio, $\lambda_E = 5$.

Table 8.2
Secant modulus of Perspex

Time after loading (mins)	Secant modulus (in lb/sq in)		
	From deflection measurements	From strain measurements	
		On tension face	On compression face
1	438,000	450,000	487,000
10	414,000	435,000	445,000
30	403,000	433,000	432,000
60	397,000	424,000	418,000

Guided by the preliminary structural dimensions provided by the consulting engineers, a scale factor of 32 was chosen, which gave a diameter of approximately 31 inches for the model. The engineers further specified a design load of 100 lb/sq ft (equal to 0·7 lb/sq inch) uniformly distributed in plan. Thus, the model load was 0·07 lb/sq inch or a total of 44 lb. This uniformly distributed load was approximated by 55 point loads. At each point the load was applied to the model by a hanger through a wire plug bearing on a thick perspex washer. Preliminary testing of the model showed that it behaved in a linear elastic fashion to a loading of at least 5 lb per load point, so a loading of 4 lb per load point reached in four 1 lb increments was considered reasonable. The loading factor was therefore $4 \times 55/44 = 5 \cdot 0$, and the observed strain and deflection readings were divided by this factor to determine the conditions in the prototype under working loads.

Deflection measurements were made with dial gauges. Strain measurements were made in part with electrical resistance strain gauges and in part with Huggenberger tensometers. The use of mechanical gauges reduces the cost, since they are recoverable; however, not all points on the model were accessible with mechanical gauges.

Assuming homogeneity of the prototype concrete structure, the tensile stresses in the model, corresponding to tensile stresses in the concrete, serve as a basis for the dimensioning of the reinforcement. Since strain measurements were generally taken at maximal points, it may be assumed that a reduction in the effective modulus of elasticity with time would result in a redistribution of stresses, leading to a reduction of peak stresses. Although strains increase with time, the maximum stresses are likely to decrease. In consequence, stresses in the dome were computed from the measured model strains on the basis of the instantaneous modulus of elasticity.

During construction a limited programme of field measurements was also undertaken. A number of reinforcing bars were instrumented with temperature-compensated electrical resistance strain gauges: care was taken during installation to protect the gauges from later moisture ingress and mechanical damage during concrete operations. By making observations before and after the striking of the formwork the effects of self-weight were obtained. Additional loading was provided by flooding the roof with water to a depth of 4 inches. Vertical deflections were measured by means of a precision level.

It is always difficult to obtain good field measurements without very elaborate preparations and procedures. However, the sense and order of magnitude of strains and displacements obtained were close to those established earlier by the model tests. For example, the largest short-term deflection predicted at the innermost compression ring was 0·45 inch, whereas that measured in the field was 0·50 inches.

A simplified statically determinate analysis was investigated by the consulting engineers and Fig. 8.6 shows a comparison of this with both model and field measurements. A large margin of strength reserve was correctly predicted by the model tests and although modifications to the design were made, it is evident that even greater refinement and economy may be achieved by testing a second model, made of micro-concrete, to enable the ultimate strength of the structure to be assessed.

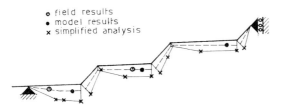

Fig. 8.6.   A comparison of the results of a simplified statically determinate analysis with the model analysis for the plated dome roof. The field measurements taken are also shown on this diagram.

8.5. *Structural Model of the Australia Square Tower**

The Australia Square Tower in Sydney was completed in 1967. It rises approximately 600 ft above its foundations, and is one of the tallest lightweight reinforced concrete buildings in the world (Fig. 8.7). It has a circular service core, which consists of an outside and inside wall interconnected by twenty radial diaphragm walls forming cells which extend the full height of the tower (Fig. 8.8). A framework of twenty tapered columns encircles this cellular core with radial beams connecting each column to the diaphragm wall opposite. The design also specifies a change in the materials; for floors below the third, a dense concrete was adopted and for floors above, a lightweight concrete.

In order to appreciate the complexity of the task of carrying out an *exact* analysis of such a structure, it is sufficient to consider that the frame is more than 12,000 fold indeterminate. It was considered

---

* *Consulting Engineers*: Civil and Civic Pty. Ltd. *Architect*: Harry Seidler.

that dead load stresses could be calculated with the desired accuracy, but stress conditions caused by wind loading needed further checking. For this purpose a structural model of sufficiently large size was built by the Department of Structural Engineering of the University of New South Wales, to enable strain and deflection measurements induced by a simulated wind loading to be measured [8.1].

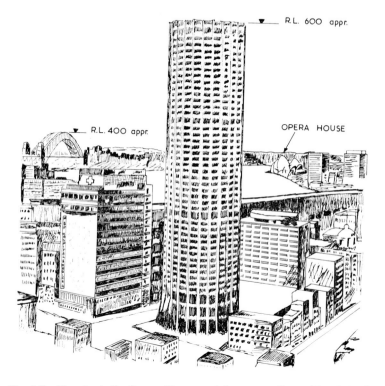

Fig. 8.7. The Australia Square Tower and its surroundings. (*Based on the original painting by Sydney artist Cedric Emanuel.*)

The intricate shapes required, such as recesses around doors; tapered columns and beams; varied slab thicknesses; the change in Young's modulus, coupled with a low Poisson's ratio, made it necessary to make the model out of a mouldable material of suitable Poisson's ratio. A *polyester casting resin* (trade name: Plastrene 97) was chosen. The elastic and other properties of this resin can be varied by using different amounts of calcite filler. The object in varying the amount of filler is to cause a change in Young's modulus of this material, and then to match the ratio of the Young's moduli for the dense and lightweight concretes of the structure with that of the model in order to fulfil the requirement of model similarity. The effect of changes in filler quantity on the material's shrinkage, coefficient of linear expansion, strength, glueability and creep characteristics had to be investigated.

The resin is a viscous liquid which readily takes up the shape of its retaining formwork and hardens at room temperature once the

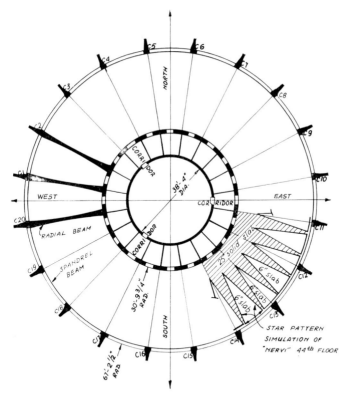

Fig. 8.8. Sectional plan of the Australia Square Tower showing double walled central service core, radial beams and external columns.

accelerator and the hardener are added to it. Setting time and the preceding rubbery stage of the Plastrene depend on the amount of accelerator used. Lift core inserts and all other formwork had to be removed in the rubbery stage before the material set hard and shrunk on to them. Complete polymerisation takes 90 days at room temperature, but elevated temperatures accelerate this process, and curing for about 3 hours at 150°F (66°C) results in full polymerisation. The most satisfactory process is to allow slow and even cooling of the heat cured components, whilst guarding them against warping. Re-heating to 180°F (84°C) softens even the fully cured material, and unwanted warps are then straightened out. The hardened product is a visco-elastic material, and in this respect is not unlike concrete.

The model was manufactured as an assembly of repetitive mass produced elements. It was possible to pour a complete floor height of the central core with all the dividing walls and openings included, if the adjoining slab was omitted. Slabs, on the other hand, could not be cast as units because of warping. Each floor slab was poured in twenty equal sectors. All components were then glued together (Fig. 8.9). Particular attention was paid to the tensile strength of the glued joints as it was always lower than the strength of the solid material.

Uniaxial tests carried out on various mixes of Plastrene indicated that strain is linearly proportional to the applied load and that Young's modulus in tension is the same as in compression.*

The static loading system consisted of twenty-eight horizontal concentrated loads simulating wind load. They were combined into a single resultant with the aid of a lever system (*Wiffle Tree*) (Fig. 8.11). Thin steel bands, flexed into a U shape to girdle the tower at the twenty-eight selected levels, provided the load transfer from the Wiffle Tree. A hydraulic jack moved the Wiffle Tree away from the tower to produce the required loading.

---

* Results of such a test conducted in 5 minutes against one that took 3 hours showed that the material remains essentially Hookean; a different Young's modulus is apparent and the difference is caused by the presence of creep strains. It is probably better to think in terms of a *reduced modulus* defined as a dimensional factor that will convert strain into stress at any particular time and temperature (Fig. 8.10).

The tower model was supported on a welded *foundation base,* consisting of a 6-ft steel plate stiffened by a two-way grid; it was bolted down to 30-ft-long interconnected girders which formed the base joists. A stiff dial gauge tower, cantilevered from the foundation

Fig. 8.9. The completed model of the Australia Square Tower. It was manufactured in segments and then glued together. The model material is a polyester casting resin—Plastrene 97.

base at the theoretical axis of bending of the model, provided the
reference axis for deflection measurements. Small, battery-operated
electric motors were attached to each of the dial gauge holders, to
eliminate by vibration false indication of the dial gauges due to
friction losses; hand tapping was too cumbersome and gave incon-
sistent results.

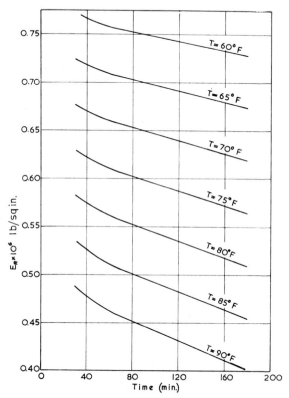

Fig. 8.10. Typical graph of reduced modulus (E_r) versus time and temperature
for plastrene 97 used for creep correction.

The model analysis was intended to establish the deflection and
stress conditions in certain parts of the structure under wind load.
More specifically, it was required to find axial forces, bending moments and shear forces in columns and beams, bending stress distri-

bution in the core, shear stress distribution in vertical planes above
door openings and in horizontal planes between two door openings
in the core. Stresses and internal actions were evaluated from strain
gauge data and deflections were measured with dial gauges.

Philips PR9812 and Kyowa linear and 45° rosette electric wire
resistance strain gauges with polyester backing were used. All were
attached with Kyowa PC–12 polyester glue which is the material used

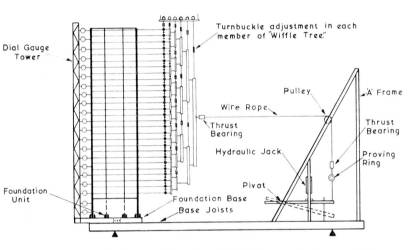

Fig. 8.11. Schematic diagram of model and Wiffle Tree loading frame: with the
movement of a single jack it is possible to apply the correct load at 28 points
concurrently.

in the model without the filler. A protective wax coating (Shell:
Micro-Wax 165) was applied, not so much to waterproof the gauges
as to prevent air streams of different temperature in the laboratory
causing temperature changes between the active and dummy
gauges. Over 500 strain gauges (linear and rosette) were attached in
the critical regions.

Testing of the tower was carried out in two stages. Stage A
represented a condition which would not occur in the prototype,
namely, a freestanding core cantilevered from the base with all slabs
attached, but before the column joints had been glued. In this condition the bending and shearing stresses can be calculated from the

simple beam theory. This gave a valuable check on the results obtained from the model and proved the validity of the method. Once the columns had been attached for the stage B tests, the model assumed the exact reduced shape of the prototype with all its complexity, and the model results could not be checked by theory. The loads were applied in four equal increments. The resulting strains were then corrected for time and temperature effects, and converted into stresses.

Data evaluation proceeded by the following steps: every entry was multiplied by a factor E_R/E_0 (where E_R is the reduced modulus at that particular time and temperature, and E_0 is the Young's modulus of Plastrene at 30 min and 75°F), which theoretically reduces the strain reading to the 30 minute value at a base temperature of 75°F (24°C); these factors were calculated from Fig. 8.10. The corrected values, giving stresses or deflections at various points of the model for a unit force, were then converted to prototype quantities using the scale factors. Typical results appear in Fig. 8.12.

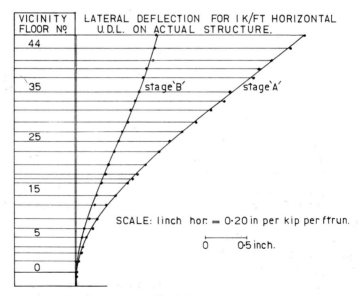

Fig. 8.12(a).

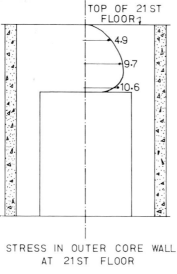

STRESS IN OUTER CORE WALL
AT 21ST FLOOR

Fig. 8.12(b).

Fig. 8.12. (a) Lateral deflections of prototype structure for a 1000 lb/ft lateral uniformly distributed load for the two basic conditions comprising stage A: central core only and stage B: central core with exterior columns and connecting radial beams plus floors. (b) Typical stress distribution in outer core wall above left door opening for 1000 lb/ft lateral uniformly distributed load with central core acting only.

8.6. *Structural Model of the Canberra Dome**

The method of support (Fig. 8.13) used for the Academy of Sciences building in Canberra introduced problems in structural analysis for which no satisfactory solutions were then available (1956). Sixteen large arches extended deep into the thin concrete dome, so that the shell was carried on sixteen supports. For preliminary design purposes a simple membrane analysis was used to proportion the dome and supports. This suggested that the form of the cut-outs would lead to a smooth introduction of direct forces into the complete dome from the reactions; but the effects of flexure

---

* *Consulting Engineers*: W. L. Irwin and Associates. *Architect*: Roy Grounds.

were less certain, as there was no reliable method for predicting the
effect of the cut-outs on shell bending.

A model [8.2], made and tested by the Department of Civil
Engineering, University of Melbourne, provided information on the
detailed stress distribution in the cut-out areas, and also gave a check
on the overall structural response of the system under various conditions of edge loading.

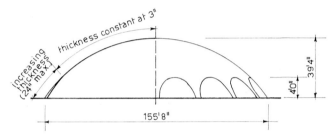

Fig. 8.13. Original design dimensions and general arrangement of the Canberra
Dome.

Many different methods of fabrication were considered. An
elastic material of known modulus was essential since stresses were
to be determined from strain measurements. Reinforced concrete
mortar was rejected because of its low elastic strain capacity in
tension and because of the difficulty of placing mortar and reinforcement in thin sections. The substantial variations in thickness
made both moulded Perspex sheet, and formed or spun metal,
impracticable.

Epoxy resin impregnated fibre-glass cloth was chosen and the
required thickness built up with a number of layers placed over a
single wooden mould in orange-peel sections. Varying orientations
were adopted in each layer to produce a reasonably isotropic structural response; subsequent behaviour confirmed that this in fact was
achieved. The model *scale* of 1:40 was a compromise between
space restrictions and the size needed for adequate strain gauging.
The completed model (Fig. 8.14) had a diameter of about 4 ft and a
crown thickness of 0·80 inches.

Instrumentation. The overall structural response of the model
was measured by dial gauges for displacements and Marten's mirrors

for relative rotations. Eighty electrical resistance strain gauges of 12 mm gauge length were used to measure upper and lower surface strains in the main shell and in the cut-out areas. In general, these were placed along and perpendicular to the meridians, but several rosette patterns were also used to determine principal stress directions in particular areas.

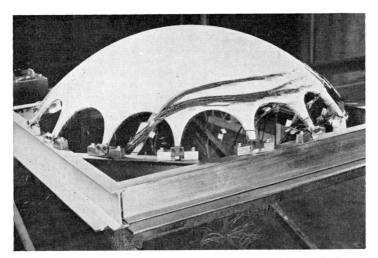

Fig. 8.14. Completed model of Canberra Dome; the model material is epoxy resin impregnated fibre glass cloth. The scale is 1 : 40.

The *resin/fibre-glass* material was found to exhibit a marked tendency to *creep* under stress. This produced a time dependent stress–strain relationship similar to the visco-elastic behaviour exhibited by Perspex. It is reasonable to consider the material as linearly elastic provided that strain readings are taken at similar time intervals after loading. Two minutes was found to be suitable, and a single value for Young's modulus of 1.75×10^6 lb/sq inch with a corresponding value of Poisson's ratio of 0.15 was adopted.

The model was loaded separately for each gauge because of problems with the switching gear.*

---

* When there is inadequate switching gear, separate loading for each gauge is a possible solution.

Several *loading conditions* were used with the model, the actions corresponding to horizontal forces and moments at the column bases being of special interest. These concentrated forces were of prime significance in the cut-out areas for actual loading conditions due to dead and live loads, shrinkage and temperature change. To apply these actions, the dome was freely supported by a small mushroom head at the crown, and the forces and moments were applied in pairs at diagonally opposite column bases. Results for any combination were then obtained by superposition.

Two typical sets of reduced *results* are reproduced in Figs. 8.15(a) and 8.15(b). Two main types of strain are of interest; meridional (or radial) and azimuthal (or circumferential). From these the corre-

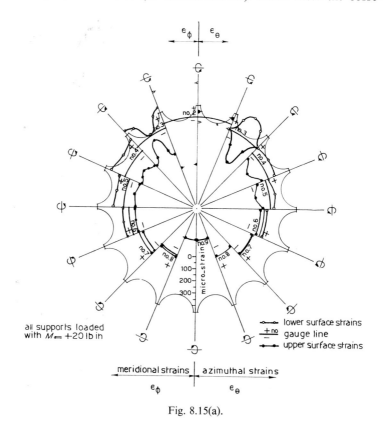

Fig. 8.15(a).

sponding stresses may be obtained using the bi-axial stress–strain relationship. The strain distributions confirmed that the influence of the cut-outs did not extend over the whole dome area. Flexural action dominated in the supports, but it was dissipated to the complete shell as membrane action, which decayed rapidly with distance from the free edge. This can be seen in Fig. 8.15(b), but it was found that the rate of decay was less over the cut-out apex than had previously been assumed in the design. Moreover, Fig. 8.15(a) indicates substantial flexural and direct circumferential stresses in this area which had not previously been suspected.

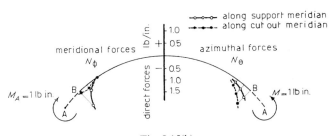

Fig. 8.15(b).

Fig. 8.15. (a) Strain distribution on the model dome for a moment equal to 20 lb/inch applied at each support. (b) Direct forces for a moment equal to 1 lb/inch at each support.

These led to modifications of the original design. The amount of reinforcement in the cut-out areas was increased and a longer thickened region was provided to give a smoother transition from the supports into the shell.

The actual structure has now been in service for nine years, and there has been no indication that the action has been significantly different from that predicted. At the present time numerical methods of analysis using digital computers could provide more detailed information about the theoretical action of a structure of this type. However, a model analysis would still be a desirable element of the investigation; partly to check the theoretical results, and partly to give the designer a feeling for the structural action.

8.7. *Model Test of Smithfield Market Shell**

In 1958 the Smithfield Poultry Market was destroyed by fire, and in the following year the design for a new market was commissioned. The proposed design was a reinforced concrete elliptical paraboloid shell roof spanning the whole market hall (Fig. 8.16). The shell is generally 3 inches thick; it has plan dimensions of 225 ft by 128 ft, and is supported around its periphery on columns mainly at 25 ft centres. For aesthetic reasons the total rise of the shell is only 30 ft so that it is flatter than any previously constructed, and buckling of the shell might be critical factor in the design. Since there was only

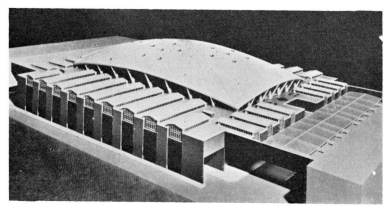

Fig. 8.16. Architectural model of the Smithfield Market (*Cement and Concrete Association, England*).

a limited amount of theory and experimental evidence available, the consultants asked the Cement and Concrete Association, London, to test a model.

This was made of reinforced micro-concrete with pre-stressed edge beams to an overall scale of 1:12. Stress and deflection distributions were investigated for a number of loading conditions, and also the buckling load [8.3].

The model was constructed by forming the supporting ribs to the basic shape and covering the area formed with two layers of $\frac{3}{16}$-inch-

---

* *Consulting Engineers*: Ove Arup and Partners. *Architect*: Sir Thomas Bennett.

thick plywood at right angles to provide stiffness. The membrane reinforcement consisted of 0·049-inch-diameter annealed drawn wire at 1-inch centres, maintained in position by passing it through slotted asbestos cement spacers. To eliminate shrinkage cracks in the membrane, it was cast in two bays separated by a central strip cast at a later date. The edge-stiffening portions and the edge beams were also cast separately. Details of the membrane reinforcement, spacers and holes for skylights can be seen in Fig. 8.17.

Fig. 8.17. The model just before casting of the micro-concrete. Details of the membrane reinforcement, spacers and sky lighting holes can be seen (*Cement and Concrete Association, England*).

The micro-concrete was made from ordinary Portland cement and a natural Thames Valley sand (sand/cement ratio 2·7; water/ cement ratio 0·47).

A reaction frame was constructed above the shell and eight air bags, especially made for the test, were then positioned between the reaction frame and the shell. Once the edge beams had been pre- stressed, the pressure in the air bags could not be allowed to fall below that required to produce stresses in the model equal to those in the prototype under the action of pre-stress and self-weight. This necessitated a continuous air supply, which also served to correct temperature variations and air leakages.

The *instrumentation* consisted of $\frac{1}{2}$-inch-long electrical resistance strain gauges in the form of 45° rosettes, arranged in 55 rosettes on both top and bottom surfaces in one quarter of the shell, a total of 330 gauges. The strains were recorded by a 100-channel recorder, and converted into stresses with a digital computer. This gave a significant reduction in the time required, and reduced the cost of evaluating the results to approximately one-sixth of the cost using an electric desk calculator. Vertical deflections were measured at 49 positions on another quarter of the shell and the edge beams, using 0·001-inch dial gauges.

Strains and deflection measurements were taken for each of seven conditions. These covered the loads on the prototype due to self-weight, uniform live load, asymmetric live load and variations in edge beam prestress. To obtain the buckling load of the shell, the corners were restrained to prevent crack propagation from the edges which, if allowed to continue unchecked, would have produced a non-buckling type of failure.

As a result of the model test the consulting engineers were supplied with information on:

(i) the magnitude of the column loads due to uniform loads and edge beam prestress,

(ii) the deflection and stress patterns due to three live load configurations and due to prestressing,

(iii) the elastic buckling load of the membrane when the corners of the roof were rigidly restrained, and

(iv) an estimate of the possible failure load of the roof with the corners unrestrained.

It was also predicted that:

(a) the shell would lift off the shuttering when the edge beams were stressed,

(b) an increase in the prestress force in the edge beams or a reduction in the self-weight of the shell would be desirable or, preferably, a combination of these two, and

(c) there would be no serious stress concentrations around skylighting holes.

8.8. *Wind-pressure Model of Toronto City Hall* *

The shell-like structure of the new Toronto City Hall rises to about 290 ft above ground level. Aerodynamically, depending on the direction of the wind, it may exhibit the flow characteristics of a diffuser, a nozzle, a semi-cylinder or a whole cylinder. The pressures exerted on the shell surfaces are expected to vary considerably as a function of the direction of the prevailing wind and may be either steady or, at specific wind directions, unsteady, *i.e.* oscillating. The sophisticated structure of the shells is inherently weak against torsional loads. The unavoidable uncertainties in any attempt to predict these loads made *wind-tunnel tests* mandatory. These were carried out by the Institute of Aerophysics of the University of Toronto [8.4]. Some changes were made in the design of the structure after the first tests were completed, and this necessitated a re-check of the aerodynamic characteristics.

The *original model* was scaled to fit inside the 36-inch by 42-inch test section of the UTIA subsonic wind tunnel. The scale of 1:276 gave a model 14·75 inches high (Fig. 8.18). It was made of solid mahogany and was mounted on a circular plywood base plate, bevelled and graduated at the outer edge. Pressure taps were located in horizontal rows at three levels on both the inside and outside walls of the large and small towers. Rows of 20 static pressure taps, spaced evenly along the arc of the tower, were built into the model wall in the following manner. A plastic strip 1 inch wide, consisting of 20 pressure tubes and running the full width of the tower, was mounted horizontally on and flush with the wall at the desired level. Each tap was formed by drilling a small hole from outside. The upstream ends of the pressure holes were plugged with pins, and the downstream ends were connected by a similar strip of tubes to a multiple manometer board.

Steady pressure measurements were taken with the tunnel running at maximum speed, about 175 ft/sec, to obtain as high a Reynolds number as possible. A typical test consisted of rotating the model slowly in the airstream through a predetermined 60° sector,

* *Consulting Engineers*: H. E. H. Roy. *Architect*: Viljo Revell, John B. Parkin Associates.

while taking readings. The same procedure was then repeated for the remaining five 60° sectors. The wind directions were kept the same for all pressure readings on a given tower within each 60° sector.

Unsteady pressures associated with periodic vortex shedding from the building were measured at four pressure taps on the outside walls located 4 inches below the top edge. These pressure taps were formed by drilling a vertical hole 4 inches deep and $\frac{5}{8}$-inch in diameter into the tower, to accommodate a microphone. Pressure was communicated from the outside to the microphone head by a small

Fig. 8.18. Wind model of the Toronto City Hall in the subsonic wind tunnel. The model is scaled down in the ratio of 1 : 276 in relation to the prototype. It is made of solid mahogany (*Institute of Aerophysics, University of Toronto*).

horizontal drill hole. To ensure undisturbed flow over the wall, the outside opening of this drill hole was closed with tape which was then punctured with a pin. The microphone was connected to a pen recorder, to a sound level meter and to an oscilloscope for immediate visual observation.

Simultaneously with the pen recordings, sound pressure level readings in decibels were taken on the sound level meter: this enabled calculation of the magnitude of the unsteady component of pressure. The frequency of vortex shedding was calculated from the pen recordings by counting the number of times the trace crossed the reference line, and dividing this number by twice the elapsed time.

Flow visualisation tests were carried out in a small smoke tunnel. The dimensions of its test section (1 inch by 12 inches) precluded testing of a model properly scaled for height. Instead, a two-dimensional model having a scale of 1:960 was used. Still photographs of the streamline pattern around the model were taken at 15° intervals in the wind direction, the wind speed being about 6 ft/sec. Furthermore, motion pictures were taken of the streamline patterns while the model was rotated through 360° in order to show the unsteady flow associated with vortex shedding at certain wind directions (Fig. 8.19).

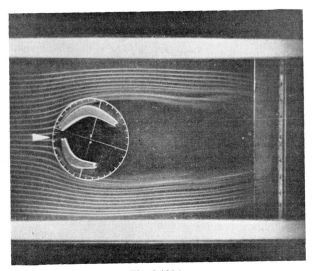

Fig. 8.19(a).

The *results* show that the steady-pressure distribution on the outside walls resembles that on a circular cylinder, with some suction peaks attaining a value of over twice the wind dynamic pressure. The outside pressure distribution is largely responsible for the torsional wind loads on the building, whereas the pressure distribution on the inside walls is uniform and contributes mainly bending.

In order to convert the wind tunnel test results into design pressures, an assumed wind velocity distribution, which varied from 110 m.p.h. at the top to 60 m.p.h. at the bottom, was used. The final prototype results of the tests produced wind pressures as high as 31 lb/sq ft and suctions as high as 72 lb/sq ft. These values, together with the unusual pressure distributions found from these tests, produced torsional and bending stresses far exceeding those which would be expected from standard design assumptions.

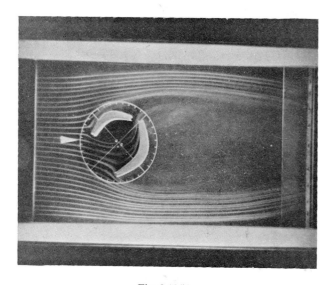

Fig. 8.19(b).

Fig. 8.19. (a) Streamline pattern of simulated steady wind conditions around a distorted two-dimensional model having a scale of 1 : 960. (b) Same model with a different orientation to wind flow, under unsteady flow: vortex shedding occurs (*Institute of Aerophysics, University of Toronto*).

The results of these tests were used in the design of the structure itself, and also in the design of supports for both the precast concrete facing panels attached to the back wall and the curtain wall construction of the interior faces of the towers.

*8.9. Model Test of a Continuous Skewed Slab Bridge**

A number of continuous skewed slab bridges were to be built in different locations, but based on the one design as the conditions of terrain and abutment separation were the same in each case. A continuous skewed slab bridge is one of the many structures for which a rigorous mathematical analysis is not available; because of the large number of bridges to be built from the one design the engineers approached the Department of Architectural Science, University of Sydney, to conduct a model analysis to verify their deflection calculations.

The bridge consisted of three approximately equal spans each of about 35 ft, set at an angle of 60° to the abutments. Whilst it would have been desirable to manufacture the model from micro-concrete in order to control Poisson's ratio, the urgency of the situation precluded its use and recourse was made to plastic as the model material.

Fig. 8.20. Continuous, three-span, skewed slab bridge model being tested for both deflection and strain using dial gauges and wire resistance strain gauges respectively.

* *Engineers*: Taylor and Herbert.

A completely similar model (Fig. 8.20) was made with a scale of 1:36 which reduced the overall size to approximately 35 inches. This scale was dictated by the thickness of commercially available plastic required to model the solid bridge deck. A 0·591 inch (15 mm) thick sheet of plastic was used with plastic crossheads, shaped to maintain the correct inertia, glued to the slab soffit above the two intermediate supporting columns. From flexure tests the elastic properties of the plastic were found to be: Poisson's ratio 0·35 and elastic modulus 0·43 × 10^6 lb/sq inch.

In order to simulate the truck loading, a single point load was applied at specified points on a predetermined grid, and influence lines for deflection drawn for each loading position. These were combined to produce the total deflection under the required loading which then consisted of a combination of the point loads. The loads were applied by a hydraulic jack through a spherical head and the deflections were measured with 1-inch-travel dial gauges. Fig. 8.21 shows a typical set of influence contours for the deflections.

The time required to complete this stage of the project was less than three weeks, and it was decided to extend the scope of the investigation to include the determination of the moments in the slab. Forty-four wire resistance strain gauges were fixed to the slab and the model was loaded again in the same manner as described above. A typical set of influence contours for strain is shown in Fig. 8.22. With surface strains known, moments in the slab were determined using the equations derived in Section 5.5.

This was a very easy model to manufacture since it could be made from sheet plastic without any shaping. The total time taken excluding the reduction of the results was less than four weeks.

8.10. Lighting Models for Subjective Studies

An example of the use of models in psychophysical experiments is the development of permanent supplementary artificial lighting by Hopkinson and Longmore at the Building Research Station, England [8.5]. Daylight alone cannot provide satisfactory lighting in many types of buildings, since it is difficult to achieve a satisfactory level of illumination at the back of a large room with a low ceiling and side windows, and to avoid discomfort glare from the sky. However, it was doubtful whether the use of artificial light alone, during daytime, was entirely satisfactory; the best solution was a proper integration of permanent supplementary artificial lighting with good

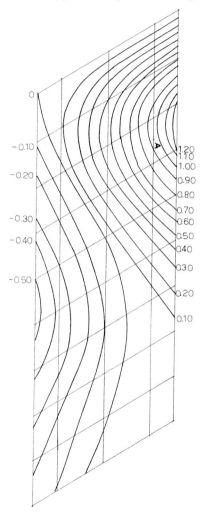

Fig. 8.21. Typical influence contours for deflection in inches at A of bridge slab.

natural lighting. The daylight is dominant; but the supplementary illumination raises the level of illumination on the visual tasks to the required value, and increases the luminance of the surrounding surfaces in the room to balance the high brightness of the external view.

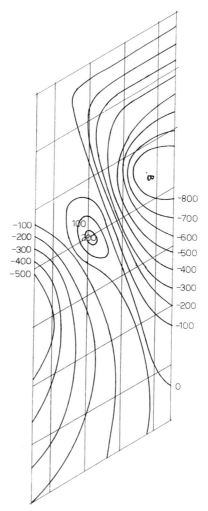

Fig. 8.22. Typical influence contours for surface strain at **B** in microstrain of model bridge slab.

Experimental work was carried out in two stages. A pilot study was made first, using a 1:12 scale model of a school room. The plan dimensions of the room were, to scale, 30 ft × 25 ft, and the ceiling height was 10 ft initially. On one side of the model room there was a window, and in the part of the room remote from the window there was a section of the ceiling that could be removed (Fig. 8.23).

The model was taken out into the open air. Six observers were then asked to look into the model, one at a time, through an aperture in one of the walls of the room at right angles to the window wall. Care was taken to ensure that the adaptation level of the observers' eyes was that of the internal brightness conditions of the model.

Fig. 8.23. Interior of the lighting model of a teaching laboratory showing the laylight and the louvred window design (*Building Research Station, England*).

Each observer was first shown the room illuminated from the side window alone. He was asked to study it in detail, noting the apparent gloominess in the parts of the room remote from the window. The section of ceiling at the back of the room was then removed, and the observer was asked to note how the additional light brightened the room and reduced the discomfort of the glare from the sky. Finally the observer was told that the object of the experiment was to see if artificial lighting could give as good a result as the roof-light and, in place of the section of ceiling that had been removed, a model laylight was installed. This consisted of two 2-ft, 40-watt fluorescent tubes in a box over a diffusing egg crate panel.

The lamps could be dimmed; the observer was given the control of the dimmer, and asked to set the variable lighting in such a way that the best balance of brightness was obtained between the different parts of the room. He was told that if the setting of the supplementary lighting were too low, then the back of the room would seem gloomy; if it were too high the double attraction of two light sources would be distressing, the side wall would vary too much in brightness, and there might be some annoyance from the excessively bright ceiling. He was asked to strike the best compromise, even though he might not be able to counteract entirely the sky glare.

After the experiment was carried out with each observer, it was entirely repeated, with the ceiling of the model sloping from 10 ft high at the laylight to 7 ft at the window wall. It was found that sky glare could not be entirely countered when there was a uniformly high ceiling. The second series of tests was intended to examine whether a reduction in the area of the sky seen by the observer would improve the balance of brightness in the room. This was found to be so.

The results of both series showed that in order to establish satisfactory conditions in the room, the level of supplementary illumination had to be high. The second stage of the programme was then entered: it involved the study of two slightly larger models, one a teaching laboratory, 36 ft × 28 ft × 10 ft high, built to 1:12 scale, and the other a research laboratory 23 ft 4 in × 10 ft by 9 ft, to 1:6 scale.

For the model teaching laboratory, a team of ten observers was used to examine the levels of artificial illumination needed to balance the brightness of the sky when seen through different window systems. The experimental technique was similar to that used earlier. Another team of thirteen observers was used to study the effect of different values of sky luminance on the level of supplementary lighting with one of these window arrangements, with that which appeared the most comfortable when there was sunlight on the window. The sky luminance visible to the observer was varied by covering the window with sheets of neutral-tinted plastic. In this set of readings, each observer was asked to image that he was working in the room and reading from the chalkboard, as well as judging the appearance of the room as a whole. He was also given the choice of whether or not to use supplementary lighting.

The model research laboratory represented a room to be used by one man. Its long narrow form was determined after a study of laboratory requirements. Six observers were asked to adjust the level of artificial lighting with three different window systems, and for three positions of the laylight. Assessment was also made of the effect of changes in the level of daylight, and of the range of external lighting conditions that were satisfactory with a fixed level of supplementary lighting.

8.11. The Measurement of Illumination and Luminance in a Model Room

The most common use of models in lighting design is the measurement of quantities of light in models of rooms for which calculation would be difficult or tedious. Fig. 8.24 shows the interior

Fig. 8.24.   Interior of a lighting model used to measure the luminance of internal surfaces and direct sunlight penetration.

of a model built in the Department of Architectural Science, University of Sydney, during a series of studies on the relative costs of different forms of lighting. Its object was to determine the exact effect of sunlight penetration through alternative window arrangements and the levels of daylighting in the room.

The prototype classroom was 26 ft × 24 ft × 9 ft 6 in high, internally, and the model was made to a scale of 1:12. The carcass of the model was $\frac{3}{8}$ inch-thick plywood; window walls were built up with $\frac{1}{8}$ inch-thick plywood mounted on acrylic sheet; the window openings were cut into the plywood. The model was finished internally by sanding, sealing the surface of the wood, and painting it with a flat, grey paint. Architraves and window frames were cut from cardboard and mounted on the windows and on the surface of the wood. The floor was covered with samples of actual vinyl asbestos tiles.

The model was first used to measure the luminance of internal surfaces when there was direct sunlight penetrating into the room. It was taken to a site outside where the conditions of surface reflectance and obstruction to light from the sky were similar to those of the prototype. Luminance measurements were made through small openings in the sides of the model, for various weather conditions and degrees of altitude and bearing of the sun, using a visual photometer. Fig. 8.25 shows a typical set of results whilst Fig. 8.24 is a photograph of the interior under the same conditions of sunlight penetration.

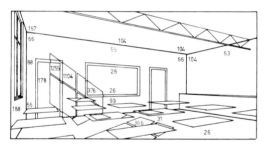

Fig. 8.25. Surface luminance levels determined from the model shown in Fig. 8.24 using a visual photometer.

Illumination in the room, from a C.I.E. Standard Overcast Sky, was measured using an artificial sky. The sky was of the mirror type, formed of a box lined internally on four sides by mirrors, and illuminated from the top by lamps over a fluorescent screen. The screen is inter-reflected among the mirrors and the effect produced is that of an infinite plane of sky. It is thus possible to produce a close approximation to the luminance distribution of the Standard Overcast Sky. The window wall of the model is placed through an opening in one of the sides of the sky. The disadvantage of this kind of sky is that the model itself is also reflected in the mirrors, producing apparently another building facing the one being studied; but this effect can be made negligible by making the sky sufficiently large. In the present case the internal dimensions of the sky enclosure were 3 ft 7 in wide and 4 ft 6 in long; the building's reflection thus appeared to be 9 ft away and gave an apparent angle of obstruction to daylight of only 2°, measured from the centre of the model's windows.

Before the model was placed in position in the sky, several cosine-corrected photo-electric cells were placed in the aperture to the sky, each one held in a shield which effectively exposed it to half a hemisphere of sky. When these cells were later put inside the model room, the daylight factor at the position of each cell was given directly by:

$$\frac{\text{current flowing from the cell in the model}}{2 \times \text{current flowing from the cell when in the sky}} \times 100\%.$$

Several forms of windows were tested, and the effects of a model venetian blind, external sun shading louvres, and curtains were examined with each one. The venetian blind was formed from the stove-enamelled slate of an actual blind, cut into strips to scale and held in a slotted metal frame; sun shading devices were formed from sheet aluminium; for the curtains, actual translucent curtain material was used, held in a rigid frame.

8.12. Airflow in Models of Industrial Buildings

In large industrial buildings in Australia it is necessary to maintain a high rate of air movement during the summer months, for air temperatures higher than 27°C frequently occur.

A detailed study was made at the Commonwealth Experimental Building Station, Sydney [8.6] to determine the best methods for increasing the speed of air flow in factories when there is a moderate wind blowing over the buildings. The investigation was confined to the provision of comfort ventilation at working level.

Model work was preceded by studies (i) of the rate of air movement required for comfort when the air temperature is high, and (ii) of the meteorological records linking wind and air temperature in the major Australian cities. These studies showed that an air speed of 200 ft/min (approximately 60 metres per minute) on hot days was required and that there was a wind of at least 4 m.p.h. (350 ft/min) for at least 90 per cent of the time when the air temperature was above 27°C in the places investigated.

A number of model structural bays of a factory were built, to 1:16 scale. The dimensions of each were, to scale, 60 ft wide × 30 ft × 15 ft high at gutters and 26 ft high at the ridge. They were made of acrylic sheet on a light wooden frame. The bays could be combined to form model factories up to 300 ft long, to scale, with either sawtooth or monitor roof forms.

A low-speed wind tunnel was used to test the models and the working section of this was approximately 20 ft long × 15 ft wide × 6 ft 6 in high. The air velocity could be varied from about $2\frac{1}{2}$ m.p.h. to 6 m.p.h. With a model in the tunnel, the direction of air movement was made visible with titanium tetrachloride smoke. The air velocity in the model was measured with thermoanemometers, and velocity in the wind tunnel outside the model with vane anemometers.

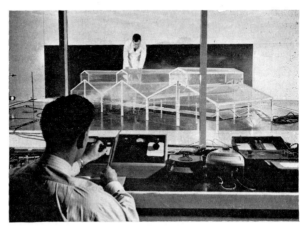

Fig. 8.26. A model factory building being tested in a low speed wind tunnel to determine airflow in industrial buildings. (*Commonwealth Experimental Building Station, Australia.*)

Two short experiments were made to test the validity of the model technique. The first was a comparison of the air flow in a model with that in a similar real building; the other was a study of the effects of varying the roughness of the ground surface. When these checks appeared satisfactory, a systematic study was made of the air flow in models with sawtooth and monitor roofs, for variations in the number and distribution of open windows, and for changes in the number and distribution of open windows, and for changes in wind direction and velocity, relative to the building. Fig. 8.26 shows the equipment being arranged for a test.

The results showed that in nearly all cases the speed of air flow through the model was greatest when the only openings were at the windward and leeward ends of the building, and when the wind was blowing in a direction perpendicular to the plane of the openings. Introduction of intermediate openings in roof-lights lowered the air velocity, reducing the efficiency of the ventilation. These findings conflict with the practice, commonly observed in factory buildings, of opening every possible window on hot days.

Bibliography

General Bibliography on Structural Models

Although structural and non-structural (*e.g.* acoustic) model investigations are occasionally described in the same paper, the literature on structural models is essentially a separate field. *The Handbook of Experimental Stress Analysis*, an encyclopaedic work with 31 contributors, covers most aspects briefly.

B.1.   M. HETENYI (Editor): *Handbook of Experimental Stress Analysis.* John Wiley, New York 1950. 1077 pp.
There are several other books on experimental stress analysis generally, but most emphasise the analysis of machine parts. Hendry is primarily concerned with the analysis of structures.

B.2.   A. W. HENDRY: *Elements of Experimental Stress Analysis.* Pergamon Press, Oxford 1964. 193 pp.
Pippard and Charlton cover two-dimensional model analysis in detail. Several books on the Theory of Structures also have a chapter on model analysis, mainly by the indirect method.

B.3.   A. J. S. PIPPARD: *The Experimental Study of Structures.* Edward Arnold, London 1947. 114 pp. (Out of print, but many libraries have copies.)

B.4.   T. M. CHARLTON: *Model Analysis of Structures.* E. & F. N. Spon, London 1954. 142 pp.
Preece and Davies describe three-dimensional model analysis.

B.5.   B. W. PREECE and J. D. DAVIES: *Models for Structural Concrete.* C. R. Books, London 1964. 252 pp.

The two classical works on photoelasticity are:

B.6.   E. G. COKER AND FILON: *A Treatise on Photoelasticity.* 2nd edn. Cambridge University Press, 1957. 720 pp.

B.7.   M. M. FROCHT: *Photoelasticity.* 2 vols. John Wiley, New York 1941 and 1946. 505 + 411 pp.
Several books contain chapters on photoelasticity, *e.g.* B1 and B2.
Many textbooks on mathematics contain chapters on dimensional analysis, and there are also specialist books on this subject.

B.8.   R. E. DOHERTY and E. G. KELL: *Mathematics of Modern Engineering.* John Wiley, New York 1936. Vol. I, Ch. 2, Sec. 5. *Dimensional Analysis*, pp. 130–163.

B.9.   D. C. IPSEN: *Units, Dimensions, and Dimensionless Numbers.* McGraw-Hill, New York 1960. 236 pp.
Several textbooks on the Theory of Structures and on the Strength of Materials contain details of analogues. Most of those useful for structural design are given in:

B.10. G. MURPHY, D. J. SHIPPY, and H. L. LUO: *Engineering Analogies.* Iowa State University Press, Ames 1963. 255 pp.

The *Proceedings of the Society for Experimental Stress Analysis* are particularly valuable for experimental techniques, but most of the papers deal with problems in mechanical engineering. The *Journal of the Structural Division* and the *Journal of the Engineering Mechanics Division* of the *American Society of Civil Engineers* contain many papers on models and analogues. The *Magazine of Concrete Research* in England and the *Architectural Science Review* in Australia have published papers particularly on three-dimensional models, and both list new publications in their bibliographical sections.

References

Chapter 2

2.1. GALILEO GALILEI LINCEO: *Discorsi e Dimostrazioni Matematiche, interno à du nuove scienze.* Elzevir, Leiden 1638. English translation by H. CREW and A. DE SALVIO, *Two New Sciences*, Macmillan, New York, 1933, p. 115.
2.2. H. J. COWAN: *An Historical Outline of Architectural Science.* Elsevier, Amsterdam, 1966, p. 35.
2.3. H. J. COWAN: *An Historical Outline of Architectural Science.* Elsevier, Amsterdam, 1966, p. 40.
2.4. C. H. GIBBONS: *Materials Testing Machines.* Instruments Publishing Company, Pittsburgh, 1935. 89 pp. (This describes the development of testing machines.)
2.5. EWART S. ANDREWS: *Elastic Stresses in Structures.* (Transl. from *Castigliano's Théorem de l'equilibre des systèmes élastiques et ses applications.*) Scott, Greenwood & Son, London, 1919. 360 pp. (*Reprinted by* Dover Publications, New York, 1966.)
2.6. C. W. CONDIT: *The Chicago School of Architecture.* University of Chicago Press, 1964. 238 pp.
2.7. G. E. BEGGS: The accurate mechanical solution of statically indeterminate structures by the use of paper models and special gauges. *J. Am. Concrete Inst.*, Vol. 18 (1922), pp. 58–78.
2.8. A. J. S. PIPPARD and S. R. SPARKES: Simple experimental solutions of certain structural design problems. *J. Inst. Civil Engs.*, Vol. 4 (1936–7), pp. 79–92.
2.9. The Müller–Breslau theorem is proved in most advanced textbooks on the Theory of Structures, *e.g.* A. J. S. PIPPARD and J. F. BAKER: *The Analysis of Engineering Structures*, 2nd edn., Edward Arnold, London, 1943, p. 357.
2.10. O. GOTTSCHALK: Mechanical calculation of elastic systems. *J. Franklin Institute*, Vol. 202 (1926), pp. 61–88.
2.11. W. J. ENEY: New deformeter apparatus. *Engineering News-Record*, Vol. 122 (16 Feb. 1939), p. 221.
2.12. M. ROCHA and J. F. BORGES: Photographic method for model analysis of structures. *Proc. Soc. Exp. Stress Analysis*, Vol. 8 (1951), No. 2, pp. 129–142.
2.13. K. H. GERSTLE and W. CLOUGH: Model analysis of three-dimensional slab structures. *Proc. Soc. Exp. Stress Analysis*, Vol. 13 (1956), No. 2, pp. 133–140.
2.14. Z. MAKOWSKI and A. J. S. PIPPARD: Experimental analysis of space structures, with particular reference to braced domes. *Proc. Inst. Civil Engs.*, Vol. 1 (1952), pp. 420–441.
2.15. E. G. COKER: Some experimental methods and apparatus for determining the stresses in bridges and framed structures. *Proc. Inst. Civil Engs.*, Vol. 229 (1929–30), pp. 33–76.
2.16. A. C. RUGE and E. O. SCHMIDT: Mechanical structural analysis by the Moment Indicator. *Proc. Am. Soc. Civil Engs.*, Vol. 64 (1938), pp. 1613–25.

2.17. C. MOSER and W. R. SCHRIEVER: Photogrammetric measurements of structures. *R.I.L.E.M. Symposium on the Observation of Structures*, Lisbon 1955, Vol. II, pp. 248–67.

2.18. G. BOWEN AND R. W. SHAFFER: Flat slab solved by model analysis. *J. Am. Concrete Inst.*, Vol. 26 (1954), pp. 553–570.

2.19. F. K. LIGTENBERG: The moiré method, a new experimental method for the determination of moments in small slab models. *Proc. Soc. Exp. Analysis*, Vol. 12 (1955), No. 2, pp. 83–92.

2.20. A. J. DURELLI AND I. M. DANIEL: Structural model analysis by means of moiré fringes. *Proc. Am. Society Civil Engs.*, Vol. 86 (1960), *J. Struct. Eng. Div.*, No. ST12, pp. 93–102.

2.21. G. DE J. DE JONG: Refraction moiré analysis of curved surfaces. *Proc. R.I.L.E.M.–I.A.S.S. Symposium on Shell Research*. North-Holland Publishing Company, Amsterdam, 1961, pp. 302–8.

2.22. J. W. DALLY, A. J. DURELLI AND W. F. RILEY: A new method to "lock-in" elastic effects for experimental stress analysis. *J. Appl. Mechanics*, Vol. 25 (1958), pp. 189–95.

2.23. F. ZANDMAN: Methode non-destructive d'analyse des contraintes par vernis photo-elastiques. (Non-destructive stress analysis with photoelastic varnishes.) *R.I.L.E.M. Symposium on the Observation of Structures*, Lisbon, 1955, Vol. II, pp. 506–25.

2.24. D. F. BILLINGTON, J. R. JANNEY AND R. MARK: Structures, models and architects. *A Seminar in Structural Model Analysis for Architectural Students*. Princeton University, Princeton, 1963. 59 pp.

2.25. S. TIMOSHENKO: *Strength of Materials*. 3rd edn. Van Nostrand, Princeton, 1955. Part I, p. 137 and p. 49.

2.26. S. TIMOSHENKO: *Strength of Materials*. 3rd edn. Van Nostrand, Princeton, 1955. Part I, p. 66.

2.27. P. L. NERVI: *Costruire Correttamente*. Hoepli, Milan, 1955. Chapter 6. *La ricerche statiche sperimentali su modelli* (Research on experimental stress analysis with models, pp. 105–113.)

2.28. *The Structures of Eduardo Torroja*. F. W. Dodge, New York, 1958. (Details of University City Hospital, Madrid, 1934, pp. 97–9.)

2.29. ISTITUTO SPERIMENTALE MODELLI E STRUTTURE: Cenni illustrativi sulle esperienze eseguite nel primo quadrennio 1951–55. (Some work of the first four years.) *Bulletin No. 3*, The Institute, Bergamo (Italy), 1955, 14 pp.

2.30. M. ROCHA: Dimensionamento experimental das estruturas. (Experimental dimensioning of structures.) *Publication No. 21*. Laboratório Nacional de Engenharia Civil, Lisbon, 1952. 71 pp.

2.31. C. BENITO: Comprobación experimental de cubiertas laminares por medio de modelos reducidos. (Experimental verification of shell roofs by means of scale models.) *Publication No. 97*. Laboratorio Central de Ensayo de Materiales de Construcción, Madrid, 1959. 38 pp.

2.32. A. L. BOUMA: Shell research in Holland. *Proceedings of the Second Symposium on Concrete Shell Roof Construction*. Teknisk Ukeblad, Oslo, 1958, pp. 284–7.

2.33. *Proceedings of a One-Day Meeting on Model Testing*. Cement and Concrete Association, London, 1964. 58 pp. (A review of work in England.)

2.34. V. A. BIKHOVSKY and others: Tests on reduced models of structures. *R.I.L.E.M. Bulletin* (Paris), No. 14 (1962), pp. 109–19. (A review of work in the U.S.S.R.)

2.35. J. E. CARPENTER, D. D. MAGURA AND N. W. HANSON: Structural model testing—techniques for models of plastic. *J. P.C.A. Res. Dev. Labs.*, Vol. 6 (1964), pp. 26–47.
2.36. H. J. COWAN: Some applications of the use of direct model analysis in the design of architectural structures. *J. Inst. Engs., Australia*, Vol. 33 (1961), pp. 259–67.
2.37. H. J. COWAN: The design of architectural structures with the aid of models. *Arch. Sci. Rev. (Sydney)*, Vol. 1 (1958). (Additional references, pp. 29–30.)
2.38. K. C. NASLUND: Model tests predict frame behaviour. *Architectural Record*, Vol. 130 (December 1961), pp. 152–4.
2.39. J. F. BAKER and others: *The Steel Skeleton.* Cambridge University Press, 1954 and 1956. 2 vol. 206 + 408 pp.
2.40. H. VOGT: Model analysis for structures in brick masonry. *R.I.L.E.M. Bull. (Paris)*, No. 8 (1960), p. 15.
2.41. P. E. SANDORFF: Design of structural models, with application to stiffened panels under combined shear and compression. *J. Aeronaut. Sci.*, Vol. 23 (1956), pp. 623–32.
2.42. J. C. CHAPMAN AND J. SLATFORD: The elastic buckling of brittle columns. *Proc. Inst. Civil Engs.*, Vol. 6 (1957), pp. 107–26.
2.43. A. L. BOUMA AND F. K. LIGTENBERG: The Philips Pavilion at the 1958 Brussels World Fair—model tests for proving the construction of the Pavilion. *Philips Tech. Rev.*, Vol. 20 (1958), pp. 17–27.
2.44. L. PRANDTL: Zur Torsion von prismatischen Stäben. (On the torsion of prismatic rods.) *Phys. Z. (Leipzig)*, Vol. 4 (1903), pp. 758–9.
2.45. A. NADAI: *Theory of Flow and Fracture of Solids.* McGraw-Hill, New York, 1950. *The problem of plastic torsion*, Vol. 1, pp. 490–511.
2.46. W. BRAY: An electrical analyser for rigid frameworks. *Struct. Engr.*, Vol. 35 (1957), pp. 297–311.
2.47. V. BUSH: Structural analysis by electrical circuit analogies. *J. Franklin Inst.*, Vol. 217 (1934), pp. 289–329.
2.48. F. L. RYDER: Application of electrical analogues of static structures. *Proc. Am. Soc. Civil Engrs.*, Vol. 85 (1959), *J. Eng. Mech.*, No. EM 1, pp. 7–32.

Chapter 3

3.1. F. L. L. CARNEIRO: Galileo, founder of the science of the strength of materials. *R.I.L.E.M. Bull.*, No. 27 (1965), pp. 99–119.
3.2. D. W. THOMPSON: *On Growth and Form.* Vols. I and II. Cambridge University Press, 1952. 1116 pp.
3.3. H. L. LANGHAAR: *Dimensional Analysis and Theory of Models.* John Wiley, New York, 1957, 166 pp.
3.4. E. BUCKINGHAM: On physically similar systems; illustrations of the use of dimensional equations. *Phys. Rev.*, Vol. IV (1914), No. 4, pp. 345–376.
3.5. S. CORRSIN: A simple geometrical proof of Buckingham's π-theorem. *Am. J. Phys.*, Vol. 19 (1951), pp. 180–182.
3.6.. N. BEAUJOINT: Similitude theory and models. *R.I.L.E.M. Bull.*, No. 7 (1960), pp. 14–39.
3.7. P. W. BRIDGMAN: *Dimensional Analysis.* Yale University Press, New Haven, 1931. 113 pp.
3.8. E. R. VAN DRIEST: On dimensional analysis and the presentation of data in fluid flow problems. *J. Appl. Mech.*, Vol. 13 (1946), No. 1, pp. 4–34.

3.9. G. MURPHY: *Similitude in Engineering*. Ronald Press, New York, 1950. 302 pp.
3.10. J. W. DUNCAN: A review of dimensional analysis. *Engineering*, Vol. 167 (1940), pp. 533–534, Vol. 167, pp. 556–557.
3.11. A. D. ROSS: Experiments on the creep of concrete under two-dimensional stressing. *Mag. Concrete Research*, Vol. 6 (1954), No. 16, pp. 3–10.
3.12. M. ROCHA: Structural model techniques—some recent developments. *Stress Analysis* (O. C. Zienkiewicz and G. S. Holister, Editors). John Wiley, New York, 1965, pp. 385–424.
3.13. E. H. BROWN AND S. L. CHOW: The photoelastic analysis of gravity stresses in shells. *Proc. World Conference on Shell Structures* 1962. National Academy of Sciences, Washington, 1964, pp. 305–310.
3.14. M. ROCHA AND J. L. SERAFIM: The use of models to determine temperature stresses in concrete arch dams. *Symposium on Concrete Dam Models*, Laboratório Nacional de Engenharia Civil, Lisbon, 1963, pp. 23.1–25.
3.15 C. MORI: Experimental determination of thermal stresses in concrete dam models. *Symposium on concrete dam models*. Laboratório Nacional de Engenharia Civil, Lisbon, 1963, pp. 1.1–16.
3.16. J. C. JONES AND D. G. THORNLEY: *Conference on Design Methods, London*, 1962, Pergamon Press, London, 1963. 222 pp.
3.17. A. B. HANDLER: The place of social science in architecture. *Arch. Sci. Rev.*, Vol. 7 (1964), pp. 129–135.
3.18. G. D. DING: Models in the design of buildings. *Arch. Sci. Rev.*, Vol. 7 (1964) pp. 48–54.

Chapter 4

4.1. LEONE BATTISTA ALBERTI: *Ten Books on Architecture* (trans. by J. Leoni), Alec Tiranti, 1955. 256 pp.
4.2. J. S. GERO, G. D. DING AND H. J. COWAN: Research in space structures. *International Conference on Space Structures*, London, 1966, Paper E3, 11 pp. (Preprint.)
4.3. H. J. COWAN: A science laboratory for architecture students. *Arch. Record*, Vol. 131, No. 3 (March 1962), pp. 145–148.
4.4. J. C. RATHBUN: Wind forces on tall buildings. *Trans. Am. Soc. Civil Eng.*, Vol. 105 (1940), pp. 1–82.
4.5. See reference 2.24.
4.6. S. TIMOSHENKO: *Strength of Materials*, Part II. Van Nostrand, Princeton, 1956, 572 pp.
4.7. E. H. BROWN: Size effects in models of structures. *Engineering*, Vol. 194 (1962), pp. 593–596.
4.8. U.S. DEPT. OF AGRICULTURE: *Wood Handbook*, Handbook No. 72. Govt. Printing Office, Washington, 1955, 528 pp.
4.9. ANON: *Properties of Plastics*. Shell Chemical Company Limited, London (undated), 13 tables.
4.10. J. F. L. FIALHO: The use of plastics for making structural models. *R.I.L.E.M. Bull.*, No. 8 (1960), pp. 65–74.
4.11. M. ROCHA: *Model Study of Structures in Portugal*. N.R.C., TT–970, National Research Council of Canada. (Translation by D. Sinclair), Ottawa, 1961, 30 pp.

214   REFERENCES

4.12. W. J. BERANEK: Models of expanded polystyrene. *Heron*, Vol. 10 (1962), pp. 80–119.
4.13. R. P. JOHNSON: Strength tests on scaled-down concretes suitable for models, with a note on mix design. *Mag. Concrete Research*, Vol. 14 (1962), pp. 47–53.
4.14. S. D. VOLKOV: *Statistical Strength Theory*. Gordon & Breach, New York, 1962. 267 pp.
4.15. Z. Y. ALAMI AND P. M. FERGUSON: Accuracy of models used in research on reinforced concrete. *Proc. Am. Concrete Inst.*, Vol. 60 (1963), pp. 1643–1663 and pp. 2067–2070.
4.16. E. FUMAGELLI: Modèles géomécaniques des reservoirs artificiels: matériaux, technique d'essais, examples de reproduction sur modèles. *Symposium on Concrete Dam Models*, Laboratório Nacional de Engenharia Civil, Lisbon, 1963, pp. 2.1–28.
4.17. G. BROCK: Direct models as an aid to reinforced concrete design. *Engineering*, Vol. 188 (1959), pp. 468–470.
4.18. J. J. RUSSELL AND F. A. BLAKEY: Physical and mechanical properties of one-cast gypsum plaster. *Aust. J. Appl. Sci.*, Vol. 7 (1956), pp. 176–190.
4.19. B. W. PREECE AND J. A. SANDOVER: Plaster models and reinforced concrete design. *Structural Concrete*, Vol. 1 (1962), pp. 148–154.
4.20. J. A. LEE AND R. C. COATES: The use of gypsum plaster as a model material. *Civil Eng. Publ. Works Rev.*, Vol. 52 (1957), pp. 1261–1263.
4.21. M. ROCHA, J. L. SERAFIM AND A. DE J. FERNANDES: Experimental studies on multiple arch dams (shells and models). *R.I.L.E.M. Bull.*, No. 11 (1961), pp. 40–51.
4.22. R. G. MATHEY AND D. WATSTEIN: Investigation of bond in beam and pull-out specimen. *Proc. Am. Concrete Inst.*, Vol. 57 (1961), pp. 1071–1090.
4.23. C. A. MENZEL AND W. M. WOODS: An investigation of bond, anchorage and related factors in reinforced concrete beams. *Portland Cement Assn.*, Bulletin No. 42, Chicago, 1952, 114 pp.
4.24. R. G. SMITH AND C. O. ORANGUN: Gypsum plaster models of unbonded prestressed concrete beams. *Civil Eng. Publ. Works Rev.*, Vol. 56 (1961), pp. 906–909 and 1061–1063.
4.25. ANON: *Machining Acrylic Materials*. I.C.I. Booklet, London (undated). 26 pp.
4.26. W. A. LITLE: *Reliability of Shell Buckling Predictions*. M.I.T. Press, Cambridge, 1964. 149 pp.
4.27. P. J. PAHL AND K. SOOSAR: *Structural Models of Architectural and Engineering Education*. M.I.T. Department of Civil Engineering Research Report, R. 64–03, Cambridge, 1964, 269 pp.

Chapter 5

5.1. T. R. CUYKENDALL AND G. WINTER: Characteristics of Huggenberger strain gauge. *Civil Eng.*, (N.Y.), Vol. 10 (1940), pp. 448–450.
5.2. A. V. HUGGENBERGER: Mechanical strain gauge technique of separating strains due to normal forces and bending moments. *Proc. Soc. Exp. Stress Analysis*, Vol. 4, No. 1 (1946), pp. 78–87.
5.3. R. A. SEFTON JENKINS: Testing of prestressed steelwork. *Conf. on the Correlation between Calculated and Observed Stresses in Structures*. Institution of Civil Engineers, London, 1955. 507 pp.

5.4. H. L. WHITTEMORE: The Whittemore strain gauge. *Instruments*, Vol. 1 (1928), pp. 299–300.

5.5. P. B. MORICE AND G. D. BASE: The design and the use of a mechanical strain gauge for concrete. *Mag. Concrete Research*, Vol. 5 (1953), pp. 37–42.

5.6. L. B. TUCKERMAN: Optical strain gauges and extensometers. *Proc. A.S.T.M.*, Vol. 23, Pt. 2 (1923), pp. 602–610.

5.7. B. L. WILSON: Characteristics of the Tuckerman strain gauge. *Proc. A.S.T.M.*, Vol. 44 (1944), pp. 1017–1026.

5.8. F. P. POTOCKI: Vibrating-wire strain gauge for long-term internal measurements in concrete. *Engineer*, Vol. 206 (1958), pp. 964–967.

5.9. J. C. CHAPMAN: Stud-welded, vibrating-wire strain gauges. *Engineer*, Vol. 206 (1958), pp. 640–641.

5.10. R. S. JERRETT: The acoustic strain gauge. *J. Sci. Instr.*, Vol. 22, No. 2 (1945), pp. 29–34.

5.11. B. C. CARTER, J. F. SHANNON AND J. R. FORSHAW: Measurements of displacement and strain by capacity methods. *Proc. Inst. Mech. Eng. (London)*,Vol. 152 (1945), pp. 215–221.

5.12. B. F. LANGER: Design and applications of magnetic strain gauge. *Proc. Soc. Exp. Stress Analysis*, Vol. 1, No. 2 (1943), pp. 82–89.

5.13. J. P. SHAMBERGER: A magnetic strain gauge. *Proc. A.S.T.M.*, Vol. 30, Pt. 2 (1930), pp. 1041–1047.

5.14. A. SCHAEVITZ: The linear differential transformer. *Proc. Soc. Exp. Stress Analysis*, Vol. 4, No. 2 (1946), pp. 79–88.

5.15. W. THOMPSON (Lord Kelvin): On the electrodynamic qualities of metals. *Phil. Trans. Roy. Soc. (London)*, Vol. 146 (1856), pp. 649–751.

5.16. E. W. KAMMER AND T. E. PARDUE: Electrical resistance changes of fine wires during elastic and plastic strains. *Proc. Soc. Exp. Stress Analysis*, Vol. 7, No. 1 (1949), pp. 7–20.

5.17. C. C. PERRY AND H. R. LISSNER: *The Strain Gauge Primer*. McGraw-Hill, New York, 1955. 281 pp.

5.18. L. M. BALL: Strain gauge technique. *Proc. Soc. Exp Stress Analysis*, Vol. 3, No. 1 (1945), pp. 1–22.

5.19. G. HONDROS AND G. J. MOORE: Strain gauges for general use in concrete. *Civil Eng. Publ. Works Rev.*, Vol. 57 (1962), pp. 756–758.

5.20. P. JACKSON: The foil strain gauge. *Instr. Practice*, Vol. 7 (1953), pp. 775–779.

5.21. C. S. SMITH: The piezoresistive effect of germanium and silicon. *Phys. Rev.*, Vol. 94 (1954), pp. 42–49.

5.22. W. P. MASON AND R. N. THURSTON: Piezo-resistive materials in measuring displacement, force and torque. *J. Acoust. Soc. Am.*, Vol. 29 (1957), pp. 1096–1101.

5.23. V. M. HICKSON: Some new techniques in strain measurement. *Stress Analysis* (O. C. Zienkiewicz and G. S. Holister, Editors). John Wiley, New York, 1965, pp. 239–263.

5.24. H. DE LEIRIS: A new pneumatic application method and its applications to extensometry. *Proc. 7th Int. Cong. App. Mech.*, London, 1948, pp. 121–127.

5.25. J. C. EVANS: Pneumatic gauging techniques. *Research (London)*, Vol. 11 (1958), pp. 90–97.

5.26. H. C. ROBERTS: Electric gauging methods: their selection and application. *Proc. Soc. Exp. Stress Analysis*, Vol. 2, No. 2 (1944), pp. 95–105.

216   REFERENCES

5.27. S. Rogers: Daisy I—a system for acquiring, analysing and plotting strain gauge data. *Proc. Soc. Exp. Stress Analysis*, Vol. 17, No. 2 (1960), pp. 87–96.
5.28. See any book on the Strength of Materials, *e.g.* ref. 2.25.
5.29. K. J. Bossart and G. A. Brewer: A graphical method of rosette analysis. *Proc. Soc. Exp. Stress Analysis*, Vol. 4, No. 1 (1946), pp. 1–8.
5.30. P. K. Stein: A simplified method of obtaining principal stress information from strain gauge rosettes. *Proc. Soc. Exp. Stress Analysis*, Vol. 15, No. 2 (1958), pp. 21–38.
5.31. W. M. Murray: Some simplifications in rosette analysis. *Proc. Soc. Exp. Stress Analysis*, Vol. 15, No. 2 (1958), pp. 39–52.
5.32. T. A. Hewson: A nomographic solution to the strain rosette equations. *Proc. Soc. Exp. Stress Analysis*, Vol. 4, No. 1 (1946), pp. 9–26.
5.33. C. H. Norris and J. B. Wilbur: *Elementary Structural Analysis*. McGraw-Hill, New York, 1960, p. 563.
5.34. F. Zandman and M. R. Wood: Photostress, a new technique for photoelastic stress analysis for observing and measuring surface strains on actual structures and parts. *Production Eng.*, Vol. 27 (Sept. 1956), pp. 167–178.
5.35. F. Zandman: Stress analysis of a guided missile tail section with the photoelastic coating technique. *Proc. Soc. Exp. Stress Analysis*, Vol. 17, No. 2 (1960), pp. 135–150.
5.36. I. Hawkes and G. S. Holister: Photoelastic techniques applied to rock mechanics problems of underground excavations and foundations. *Stress Analysis* (O. C. Zienckiewicz and G. S. Holister, Editors), John Wiley, New York, 1965, pp. 264–292.
5.37. D. Drucker: Photoelastic separation of principal stress by oblique incidence. *J. Appl. Mech.*, Vol. 10, No. 3 (1943), pp. A156–A160.
5.38. D. Drucker: The method of oblique incidence in photoelasticity. *Proc. Soc. Exp. Stress Analysis*, Vol. 8, No. 1 (1950), pp. 51–66.
5.39. F. Zandman, S. S. Redner and E. I. Riegner: Reinforcing effects of birefringent coatings. *Exp. Mech.*, Vol. 2, No. 2 (1962), pp. 55–64.
5.40. D. Post and F. Zandman: Accuracy of birefringent-coating method for coatings of arbitrary thickness. *Proc. Soc. Exp. Stress Analysis*, Vol. 18, No. 1 (1961), pp. 21–32.
5.41. F. Leonhardt and W. Andra: A simple method to draw influence lines for slabs. *R.I.L.E.M. Bull.*, No. 11 (1961), pp. 25–29.
5.42. H. Schenck: *Theories of Engineering Experimentation*. McGraw-Hill, New York, 1961. 239 pp.
5.43. A. J. Durelli, E. A. Phillips and C. H. Tsao: *Introduction to the Theoretical and Experimental Analysis of Stress and Strain*. McGraw-Hill, New York, 1958, p. 120 and p. 141.
5.44. A. M. Neville and J. B. Kennedy: *Basic Statistical Methods for Engineers and Scientists*, International Textbook Co., Scranton (Penn.), 1964. 325 pp.
5.45. J. E. Freund: *Mathematical Statistics*. Prentice-Hall, New York, 1962. 390 pp.
5.46. A. Hald: *Statistical Theory with Engineering Applications*. John Wiley, New York, 1952. 783 pp.
5.47. R. A. Fisher: *Statistical Methods for Research Workers*. Hafner, New York, 1946. 354 pp.
5.48. B. Ostle: *Statistics in Research*. Iowa University Press, Ames, 1963. 585 pp.

Chapter 6

6.1. A. J. BUTLER: Model design techniques. *J. Inst. Heating Vent. Engrs.*, Vol. 31 (1964), pp. 401–406.
6.2. H. J. COWAN: The architectural science laboratory of the University of Sydney. *Arch. Sci. Rev.*, Vol. 4 (1961), pp. 58–83.
6.3. W. G. GODDEN: *Demonstration Models for Teaching Structural Mechanics.* University of Illinois Engineering Experimental Station, Circular No. 78, Urbana, 1962. 84 pp.

Chapter 7

7.1. R. W. R. Muncey AND J. W. SPENCER: Calculations of non-steady heat flow: considerations of radiation within the room. *J. Inst. Heating Vent. Engrs.*, Vol. 34 (1966), pp. 35–38.
7.2. L. G. ALEXANDER: *Theory and Construction of Thermal Models of Buildings.* Australian Commonwealth Experimental Station, Special Report No. 4, Sydney, 1949. 178 pp.
7.3. J. W. DRYSDALE: *The Thermal Behaviour of Dwellings.* Australian Commonwealth Experimental Building Station, Tech. Study 34, Sydney, 1950. 42 pp.
7.4. V. PASCHKIS AND H. D. BAKER: A method for determining unsteady-state heat transfer by means of an electrical analogy. *Trans. Am. Soc. Mech. Eng.*, Vol. 64 (1942), pp. 105–112.
7.5. N. S. BILLINGTON: The use of electrical analogies in heating research. Building Research Congress 1951, London, Paper Division 3, pp. 75–81.
7.6. C. S. LEOPOLD: Hydraulic analogue for the solution of problems of thermal storage, radiation, convection and conduction. *Heating, Piping Air Condit.*, Vol. 20 (1948), pp. 105–111.
7.7. E. DANTER: Recent work on heating and ventilation at the Building Research Station. *J. Inst. Heating Vent. Engrs.*, Vol. 31 (1963–64), pp. 42-45.
7.8. G. M. DUSINBERRE: *Numerical Analysis of Heat Flow.* McGraw-Hill, New York, 1949. 227 pp.
7.9. A. H. VAN GORCUM: Theoretical considerations on the conduction of fluctuating heat flow. *Appl. Sci. Res. (The Hague)*, Vol. A2, No. 4 (1950), pp. 272–280.
7.10. R. W. R. MUNCEY: The calculation of temperatures inside buildings having variable external conditions. *Aust. J. Appl. Sci.*, Vol. 4 (1953), pp. 189–196.
7.11. L. A. PIPES: Matrix analysis of heat transfer problems. *J. Franklin Inst.*, Vol. 263 (1957), pp. 195–206.
7.12. A. F. B. NICKSON AND R. W. MUNCEY: The listener and measurements in and criteria for room acoustics. *J. Sound Vibr.*, Vol. 1 (1964), pp. 141–147, 148–156, 292–297.
7.13. L. L. BERANEK: *Music, Acoustics and Architecture.* John Wiley, New York (1962). 586 pp.
7.14. A. F. B. NICKSON AND R. W. MUNCEY: Some experiments in a room and its acoustic model. *Acustica*, Vol. 6 (1956), pp. 295–302.
7.15. A. K. CONNOR: Models as an aid in the acoustical design of auditoria. *Acustica*, Vol. 9 (1959), pp. 403–407.

Chapter 8

8.1. P. S. BALINT AND F. S. SHAW: Structural model of the Australia Square Tower in Sydney. *Arch. Sci. Rev.*, Vol. 8 (1965), pp. 136–149.

8.2. L. K. STEVENS: Investigations on a model dome with arched cut-outs. *Mag. Concrete Res.*, Vol. 11 (1959), pp. 3–14.

8.3. L. L. JONES AND G. D. BASE: Test on a one-twelfth scale model of the dome shell roof for Smithfield Poultry Market. *Proc. Inst. Civil Engrs.*, Vol. 30 (1965), pp. 109–130.

8.4. K. DAU: *Wind Tunnel Tests of the Toronto City Hall*. University of Toronto, Inst. of Aerophysics, Tech. Note No. 50. 48 pp.

8.5. R. G. HOPKINSON: *Architectural Physics—Lighting*. H.M. Stationery Office, London, 1963, pp. 296–318.

8.6. E. T. WESTON: *Natural Ventilation in Industrial-type Buildings*. Australian Commonwealth Experimental Building Station, Special Report No. 14, Sydney, 1954. 47 pp.

Nomenclature

A	area of cross-section; or sound absorption coefficient
a	acceleration; or distance; or exponent of dimension
b	width of rectangular section; or thermal absorptivity; or exponent of dimension
C	specific heat; or constant of proportionality
C_ε	strain optical coefficient
C_σ	stress optical coefficient
c	velocity of sound in air; or exponent of dimension
d	depth of section
E	direct modulus of elasticity (Young's modulus)
F	dimension of force
$F_{1,2,3}$	dimensionally homogeneous function
f	frequency of vibration; or material fringe value
G	modulus of elasticity in shear (modulus of rigidity)
g	acceleration due to gravity
h	surface film conductance
I	moment of inertia (second moment of area); or electric current; or incident radiation
J	polar moment of inertia
$K_{a,b,s,t}$	constants accounting for relative effects of axial force, bending moment, shear force and torsional moment, respectively
k	thermal conductivity; or constant
L	dimension of length
l	length; or span
M	dimension of mass
M	bending moment
M_w	statically determinate bending moment
M_r	statically indeterminate bending moment
m	constant slope of the sand heap; or mass
m	*as subscript denotes* model
M_x	bending moment about x-axis
M_y	bending moment about y-axis
M_{xy}	twisting moment
$M_{1,2}$	bending moment about principal axis

219

M_{45}	bending moment at 45° to axis
N_x	force normal to y-axis
N_y	force normal to x-axis
N_{xy}	shear force
n	fringe order
P	axial force
p	pressure
p	*as subscript denotes* prototype
R	reaction; or resistance
R_x	radius of curvature in the x-direction
R_y	radius of curvature in the y-direction
r	radius of reinforcement; or relative retardation
S	area
T	dimension of time
T	tension
T_s	sol-air temperature
T_a	shade air temperature
t	time; or thickness
u	displacement in the x-direction; or bond strength; or temperature
V	volume; or voltage
v	shear stress; or displacement in the y-direction; or velocity
W	load, force
w	displacement in the z-direction
x, y, z	orthogonal co-ordinates
y	deflection
Z	modulus of section
z	transverse deflection
α	coefficient of expansion; or coefficient of expansion of gauge material; or exponent of dimension
β	coefficient of expansion of gauge mounting material; or exponent of dimension
γ	specific weight; or exponent of dimension
γ_{xy}	shear strain
Δ	sidesway displacement
δ	displacement
ε	strain
ε_θ	strain in direction defined by the angle θ

$\varepsilon_{1,2}$	strain in the principal directions
$\varepsilon_{x,y,z}$	strain in three orthogonal directions
η	thermal coefficient of resistivity
θ	angle; or dimension of temperature
κ	thermal diffusivity
λ	scale ratio; or wave length
μ	Poisson's ratio
ρ	specific mass (density)
σ	stress
$\sigma_{x,y,z}$	stress in three orthogonal directions
τ	angle of twist; or shear stress
Φ	elastic torsion function
ϕ	angle
χ_x	change in curvature in the x-direction
χ_y	change in curvature in the y-direction
Ψ	plastic torsion function

Conversion Factors

To convert	Into	Multiply by
Btu	joules	1,054·8
cubic feet	cu metres	0·02832
cubic inches	cu cm	16·39
Fahrenheit	Centigrade	$(F° - 32) \times 5/9$
feet	centimetres	30·48
inches	centimetres	2·540
mph	km/h	1·609
lb/sq ft	kg/sq metre	4·882
lb/sq in	kg/sq metre	703·1
tons	kilogrammes	1,016·0

Index

Absorption coefficient, 153
Acceleration, 40, 57
Acceleration similarity, 55
Acclimatization, 142
Accuracy, 93
Acoustical analogues, 154
Acoustical comfort, 144
Acoustical environment, 153
Acoustic model, 2, 63, 155
Acoustical strain gauge, 99
Acrylic plastic, 23, 85
Active gauge, 107
Adaptation level, 201
Air bag loading, 125, 191
Air-conditioning services, 136
Air flow, 136, 205
Air movement, 143
Alberti, Leone, 65
Analogues, 4, 24, 30, 145
Analyser, 117
Area, 46
Artificial lighting, 201
Artificial sky, 159, 204
Asbestos cement sheet, 82
Auditoria, 153
Automatic recording, 111
Automatic switching, 110

Balsa wood, 66, 135
Basic dimensions, 37, 39
Beggs, G.E., 3, 8
Behavioural models, 66
Birefringent plastic, 116
Bond strength, 84
Bonded-foil strain gauge, 103
Bonded-wire strain gauge, 102
Boundary conditions, 164
Brass, 138

Bray equation, 32
Brewster, Sir David, 17
Brightness, 202
Brittle coatings, 21
Buckingham π-theorem, 44
Bush equation, 31
Buckling, 7, 24, 172, 192

Calcite filler, 179
Capacitance strain gauge, 100
Castigliano, Carlo, 8
Casting resin, 18, 24, 175, 178
Celluloid, 18
Cellulose-based adhesives, 105
Cementing, 87
Centrifugal forces, 127
Circumferential strains, 188
Classroom demonstration models, 139
Clay, 136
Coefficient of expansion similarity, 55
Coker, E. G., 17
Column effective length, 171
Comfort, 142
Computer programs, 5, 12, 33, 111, 168
Conduction, 147
Confirmatory models, 67
Construction of models, 66, 85
   Assembly, 87
   Casting, 90
   Cementing, 87
   Cut-out techniques, 85
   Mechanical jointing, 87
   Spin forming, 92
   Thermal forming, 88